Global Economic History: A Very Short Introduction

VERY SHORT INTRODUCTIONS are for anyone wanting a stimulating and accessible way in to a new subject. They are written by experts and have been translated into more than 40 different languages. The series began in 1995 and now covers a wide variety of topics in every discipline. The VSI library contains nearly 400 volumes—a Very Short Introduction to everything from Indian philosophy to psychology and American history—and continues to grow in every subject area.

Very Short Introductions available now:

ACCOUNTING Christopher Nobes
ADVERTISING Winston Fletcher
AFRICAN HISTORY John Parker and
    Richard Rathbone
AGNOSTICISM Robin Le Poidevin
ALEXANDER THE GREAT
    Hugh Bowden
AMERICAN HISTORY Paul S. Boyer
AMERICAN IMMIGRATION
    David A. Gerber
AMERICAN POLITICAL PARTIES
    AND ELECTIONS L. Sandy Maisel
AMERICAN POLITICS Richard M. Valelly
THE AMERICAN PRESIDENCY
    Charles O. Jones
ANAESTHESIA Aidan O'Donnell
ANARCHISM Colin Ward
ANCIENT EGYPT Ian Shaw
ANCIENT GREECE Paul Cartledge
THE ANCIENT NEAR EAST
    Amanda H. Podany
ANCIENT PHILOSOPHY Julia Annas
ANCIENT WARFARE Harry Sidebottom
ANGELS David Albert Jones
ANGLICANISM Mark Chapman
THE ANGLO-SAXON AGE John Blair
THE ANIMAL KINGDOM Peter Holland
ANIMAL RIGHTS David DeGrazia
THE ANTARCTIC Klaus Dodds
ANTISEMITISM Steven Beller
ANXIETY Daniel Freeman and
    Jason Freeman
THE APOCRYPHAL GOSPELS
    Paul Foster
ARCHAEOLOGY Paul Bahn

ARCHITECTURE Andrew Ballantyne
ARISTOCRACY William Doyle
ARISTOTLE Jonathan Barnes
ART HISTORY Dana Arnold
ART THEORY Cynthia Freeland
ASTROBIOLOGY David C. Catling
ATHEISM Julian Baggini
AUGUSTINE Henry Chadwick
AUSTRALIA Kenneth Morgan
AUTISM Uta Frith
THE AVANT GARDE David Cottington
THE AZTECS David Carrasco
BACTERIA Sebastian G. B. Amyes
BARTHES Jonathan Culler
THE BEATS David Sterritt
BEAUTY Roger Scruton
BESTSELLERS John Sutherland
THE BIBLE John Riches
BIBLICAL ARCHAEOLOGY Eric H. Cline
BIOGRAPHY Hermione Lee
THE BLUES Elijah Wald
THE BOOK OF MORMON Terryl Givens
BORDERS Alexander C. Diener and
    Joshua Hagen
THE BRAIN Michael O'Shea
THE BRITISH CONSTITUTION
    Martin Loughlin
THE BRITISH EMPIRE Ashley Jackson
BRITISH POLITICS Anthony Wright
BUDDHA Michael Carrithers
BUDDHISM Damien Keown
BUDDHIST ETHICS Damien Keown
CANCER Nicholas James
CAPITALISM James Fulcher
CATHOLICISM Gerald O'Collins

Robert C. Allen

GLOBAL ECONOMIC HISTORY

A Very Short Introduction

OXFORD
UNIVERSITY PRESS

Great Clarendon Street, Oxford ox2 6DP

Oxford University Press is a department of the University of Oxford.
It furthers the University's objective of excellence in research, scholarship,
and education by publishing worldwide in

Oxford New York

Auckland Cape Town Dar es Salaam Hong Kong Karachi
Kuala Lumpur Madrid Melbourne Mexico City Nairobi
New Delhi Shanghai Taipei Toronto

With offices in

Argentina Austria Brazil Chile Czech Republic France Greece
Guatemala Hungary Italy Japan Poland Portugal Singapore
South Korea Switzerland Thailand Turkey Ukraine Vietnam

Oxford is a registered trade mark of Oxford University Press
in the UK and in certain other countries

Published in the United States
by Oxford University Press Inc., New York

© Robert C. Allen 2011

British Library Cataloguing in Publication Data
Data available

Library of Congress Cataloging in Publication Data
Data available

Typeset by SPI Publisher Services, Pondicherry, India
Printed in Great Britain
on acid-free paper by
Ashford Colour Press Ltd, Gosport, Hampshire

ISBN: 978–0–19–959665–2

7 9 10 8

Contents

Acknowledgements

I am grateful to the people who worked with me as research assistants in reconstructing the wage and price history of the world – Stuart Murray, Cherie Metcalfe, Ian Keay, Alex Whalley, Victoria Bateman, Roman Studer, Tommy Murphy, and Eric Schneider. Their attention to detail as well as their thoughts on the project and the text were invaluable to me. I also thank many friends who read earlier drafts and discussed these issues with me: Paul David, Larry Eldredge, Stan Engerman, James Fenske, Tim Levnig, Roger Goodman, Phil Hoffman, Chris Kissane, Peter Lindert, Branko Milanovic, Patrick O'Brien, Gilles Postel-Vinay, Jim Robinson, Jean-Laurent Rosenthal, Ken Sokoloff, Antonia Strachey, Francis Teal, Peter Temin, Jan Luiten van Zanden, Lawrence Whitehead, Jeff Williamson, and Nick Woolley. My son Matthew Allen and my wife Dianne Frank were cheerful and supportive despite my obsessive attention to this project and countless requests to comment on drafts. It is a better book for their reading.

I am pleased to acknowledge many years of research funding from the Canadian Social Sciences and Humanities Research Council and the United States National Science Foundation through the Global Price and Income History Group.

I dedicate the book to my son Matthew, and to other members of his generation, in the hope that understanding how the world has come to be as it is will help them make it better.

List of illustrations

List of tables

Chapter 1
The great divergence

Economic history is the queen of the social sciences. Her subject is *The Nature and Causes of the Wealth of Nations*, the title of Adam Smith's great book. Economists seek the 'causes' in a timeless theory of economic development, while economic historians find them in a dynamic process of historical change. Economic history has become particularly exciting in recent years since the scope of the fundamental question – 'why are some countries rich and others poor?' – has gone global. Fifty years ago, the question was 'why did the Industrial Revolution happen in England rather than France?' Research on China, India, and the Middle East has emphasized the inherent dynamism of the world's great civilizations, so today we must ask why economic growth took off in Europe rather than Asia or Africa.

Data on incomes in the distant past are not robust, but it looks as though the differences in prosperity between countries in 1500 were small. The present division between rich and poor largely emerged since Vasco da Gama sailed to India and Columbus discovered the Americas.

We can divide the last 500 years into three periods. The first, which lasted from 1500 to about 1800, was the *mercantilist era*. It began with the voyages of Columbus and da Gama, which led to an integrated global economy, and ended with the Industrial Revolution. The Americas were settled and exported silver, sugar, and tobacco; Africans were shipped as slaves to the Americas to produce these goods; and Asia sent spices, textiles, and porcelain to Europe. The leading European countries sought to increase their trade by acquiring colonies and using tariffs and war to prevent other countries from trading with them. European manufacturing was promoted at the expense of the colonies, but economic development, as such, was not the objective.

This changed in the second period of *catch-up* in the 19th century. By the time Napoleon was defeated at Waterloo in 1815, Britain had established a lead in industry and was out-competing other countries. Western Europe and the USA made economic development a priority and tried to achieve it with a standard set of four policies: creation of a unified national market by eliminating internal tariffs and building transportation infrastructure; the erection of an external tariff to protect their industries from British competition; the chartering of banks to stabilize the currency and finance industrial investment; and the establishment of mass education to upgrade the labour force. These policies were successful in Western Europe and North America, and the countries in these regions joined Britain to form today's club of rich nations. Some Latin American countries adopted these policies incompletely and without great success. British competition de-industrialized most of Asia, and Africa exported palm oil, cocoa, and minerals once the British slave trade was ended in 1807.

In the 20th century, the policies that had worked in Western Europe, especially in Germany, and the USA proved less effective in countries that had not yet developed. Most technology is invented in rich countries, and they develop technologies that use more and more capital to increase the productivity of their ever more expensive labour. Much of this new technology is not cost-effective in low-wage countries, but it is what they need in order to catch up to the West. Most countries have adopted modern technology to some degree, but not rapidly enough to overtake the rich countries. The countries that have closed the gap with the West in the 20th century have done so with a *Big Push* that has used planning and investment coordination to jump ahead.

Before we can learn *how* some countries became rich, we must establish *when* they became rich. Between 1500 and 1800, today's rich countries forged a small lead that can be measured in terms of GDP (gross domestic product) per person (Table 1). In 1820, Europe was already the richest continent. GDP per head was twice that of much of the world. The most prosperous country was the Netherlands, with an average income (GDP) of $1,838 per person. The Low Countries had boomed in the 17th century, and the main question of economic policy elsewhere was how to catch up with the Dutch. The British were doing that. The Industrial Revolution had been under way for two generations, and Great Britain was the second richest economy, with an income of $1,706 in 1820. Western Europe and Britain's offshoots (Canada, Australia, New Zealand, and the USA) had incomes of between $1,100 and $1,200. The rest of the world lagged behind, with per capita incomes between $500 and $700. Africa was the poorest continent at $415.

Between 1820 and the present, the income gaps have expanded with only a few exceptions. The countries that were richest in 1820 have grown the most. Today's rich countries have average incomes of $25,000–$30,000, much of Asia and Latin America average $5,000–$10,000, while sub-Saharan Africa has reached only $1,387. The phenomenon of divergence is highlighted in Figure 1, in which the regions plotted towards the right with higher incomes in 1820 had the greatest income growth factors, and the regions on the left with lower initial incomes had smaller growth factors. Europe and the British offshoots realized income gains of 17- to 25-fold. Eastern Europe and much of Asia started

Table 1. GDP per person around the world, 1820–2008

	1820	1913	1940	1989	2008
Great Britain	1706	4921	6856	16414	23742
Netherlands	1838	4049	4832	16695	24695
Other Western Europe	1101	3608	4837	16880	21190
Mediterranean Europe	945	1824	2018	11129	18218
Northern Europe	898	2935	4534	17750	25221
USA, Canada, NZ, Australia	1202	5233	6838	21255	30152
Eastern Europe	683	1695	1969	5905	8569
USSR	688	1488	2144	7112	7904
Argentina, Uruguay, Chile	712	3524	3894	6453	8885

	1820	1913	1940	1989	2008
Other Latin American countries	636	1132	1551	4965	6751
Japan	669	1387	2874	17943	22816
Taiwan & S Korea	591	835	1473	8510	20036
China	600	552	562	1834	6725
Indian Sub-continent	533	673	686	1232	2698
Other east Asia	562	830	840	2419	4521
Middle East & North Africa	561	994	1600	3879	5779
Sub-Saharan Africa	415	568	754	1166	1387
World	666	1524	1958	5130	7614

GDP measures the total output of goods and services in an economy as well as the total income generated by it. In this table, GDP is valued in 1990 US dollars so the volume of production (real income) can be compared over time and across space.

Note: Great Britain includes Northern Ireland from 1940

5

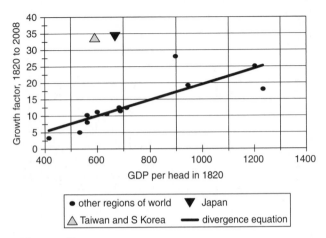

1. The great divergence

with lower incomes and realized increases of 10-fold. South Asia, the Middle East, and much of sub-Saharan Africa were less fortunate, being both poorer in 1820 and achieving income gains of only 3- to 6-fold. They have fallen even further behind the West. The 'divergence equation' summarizes this pattern.

There are exceptions to income divergence. East Asia is the most important, for it is the one region that bucked the trend and improved its position. Japan was the greatest success of the 20th century, for it was indubitably a poor country in 1820 and yet managed to close the income gap with the West. Equally dramatic has been the growth of South Korea and Taiwan. The Soviet Union was another, although less complete, success. China may be repeating the trick today.

Industrialization and de-industrialization have been major causes of the divergence in world incomes (Figure 2). In 1750, most of the world's manufacturing took place in China (33% of the world total) and the Indian subcontinent (25%). Production per person was

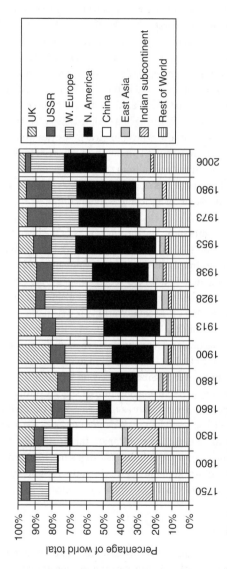

2. **Distribution of world manufacturing**

lower in Asia than in the richer countries of Western Europe, but the differentials were comparatively small. By 1913, the world had been transformed. The Chinese and Indian shares of world manufacturing had dropped to 4% and 1% respectively. The UK, the USA, and Europe accounted for three-quarters of the total. Manufacturing output per head in the UK was 38 times that in China and 58 times that in India. Not only had British output grown enormously, but manufacturing had declined absolutely in China and India as their textile and metallurgical industries were driven out of business by mechanized producers in the West. In the 19th century, Asia was transformed from the world's manufacturing centre into classic underdeveloped countries specialized in the production and export of agricultural commodities.

Figure 2 highlights some key turning points in the history of the world. From 1750 to 1880, the British Industrial Revolution was the major event. In this period, Britain's share of world manufacturing increased from 2% to 23%, and it was British competition that destroyed traditional manufacturing in Asia. The period from 1880 to the Second World War was marked by the industrialization of the USA and continental Europe including Germany, in particular. Their shares reached 33% and 24%, respectively, in 1938. Britain lost ground to these competitors, and its share dropped to 13%. Since the Second World War, the USSR's share of world manufacturing output rose sharply until the 1980s and then crashed precipitously as the post-Soviet countries went into economic decline. The East Asian miracle saw a rise in the share of world manufacturing in Japan, Taiwan, and South Korea to 17%. China has also been industrializing since 1980, and produced 9% of world manufactures in 2006. If China catches up to the West, the world will have come full circle.

Real wages

GDP is not an adequate measure of wellbeing. It leaves out many factors such as health, life expectancy, and educational attainment. In addition, absence of data often makes GDP hard to compute, and, in any event, it may be misleading because it averages the incomes of the rich with the poor. These problems can be finessed by calculating 'real wages', that is, the standard of living that can be bought with one's earnings. Real wages tell us much about the standard of living of the average person and help explain the origins and spread of modern industry, for the incentive to increase the amount of machinery used by each worker is greatest where labour is dearest.

I focus on labourers. To measure their standard of living, their wages must be compared to the prices of consumer goods, and those prices must be averaged to calculate a consumer price index. My index is the cost of maintaining a man at 'bare-bones subsistence' (the least-cost way of staying alive). The diet is quasi-vegetarian. Boiled grain or unleavened bread provide most of the calories, legumes are a protein-rich complement, and butter or vegetable oil provides a little fat. This was typical fare around the world in 1500. Francisco Pelsaert, a Dutch merchant who visited India in the early 17th century, observed that the people near Delhi 'have nothing but a little kitchery [kedgeree] made of green pulse mixed with rice ... eaten with butter in the evening, in the day time they munch a little parched pulse or other grain'. The workmen 'know little of the taste of meat'. Indeed, most meats were taboo.

Table 2 shows the consumption pattern defining bare-bones subsistence for an adult male. The diet is based on the cheapest grain available in each part of the world – oats in northwestern Europe, maize in Mexico, millet in northern India, rice in coastal China, and so on. The quantity of the grain is chosen, so that the diet yields 1,940 calories per day. Non-food spending is restricted to scraps of cloth, a bit of fuel, and the odd candle. Most spending is on food, and, indeed, on the carbohydrate at the core of the diet.

The fundamental standard of living question is whether a fully employed labourer earned enough to support a family at bare-

Table 2. Bare-bones subsistence basket of goods

	quantity per man per year	calories per day	protein (grams) per day
food			
grain	167 kg	1657	72
beans	20 kg	187	14
meat	5 kg	34	3
butter	3 kg	60	0
total		1938	89
non-food			
soap	1.3 kg		
linen/cotton	3 metres		
candles	1.3 kg		
lamp oil	1.3 litres		
fuel	2.0 Million British Thermal Units		

Note: The table is based on quantities and nutritional values for the oatmeal diet of north/western Europe. For other parts of the world, the diet uses the cheapest available grain, and the exact quantities consequently vary.

bones subsistence. Figure 3 shows the ratio of full-time earnings to the family's cost of subsistence. Today, living standards are similar across Europe. The 15th century was the last time that was true. Living standards then were also high: labourers earned about four times bare-bones subsistence. By the 18th century, however, a great divergence had occurred in Europe. The standard of living on the continent collapsed, and labourers earned only enough to purchase the items in Table 2 or equivalent. In the Middle Ages, Florentine workers ate bread, but by the 18th

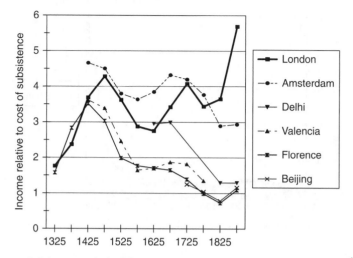

3. Subsistence ratio for labourers

century they could afford only polenta made from maize, newly introduced from the Americas.

In contrast, labourers in Amsterdam and London still earned four times bare-bones subsistence. Workers in London in 1750 did not, however, eat four times the oatmeal specified in Table 2. Instead, they upgraded their diet to white bread, beef, and beer. It was only on the Celtic fringe that the British ate oats. As Doctor Johnson remarked, oats are 'a grain which in England is generally given to horses but in Scotland supports the people'. The workers of southern England also had the income to purchase the luxuries of the 18th century such as the odd book, a mirror, sugar, or tea.

Real wages have diverged as dramatically as GDP per head. Figure 4 shows the real wage of labourers in London from 1300 to the present and in Beijing from 1738. In 1820, the London real wage was already four times subsistence, and the ratio has grown to fifty – mainly since 1870.

11

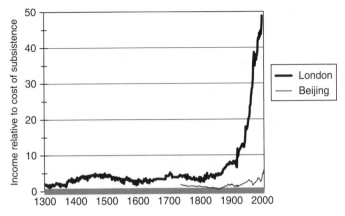

4. Subsistence ratio, London and Beijing

In the poor countries of the world, however, real wages are still at bare-bones subsistence. In 1990, the World Bank defined a world poverty line at $1 per day (since raised to $1.25 due to inflation). This figure, which is based on the poverty lines of present-day poor countries, corresponds to bare-bones subsistence as defined in Table 2. Those baskets averaged $1.30 per person per day when priced in 2010. More than one billion people (15% of the world's population) live below that line today, and the proportion was far higher in 1500. Labourers in Beijing were this poor in the 19th century. China's remarkable growth in recent decades has boosted the labourer's standard of living to only six times subsistence – a level that British workers realized 150 years ago.

We can now appreciate the low incomes shown in Table 1 for 1820. They are expressed in 1990 dollars, and, at that time, bare-bones subsistence cost $1 per day or $365 per year. Average income in sub-Saharan Africa in 1820 was $415 – only 15% more than bare-bones subsistence, which was the standard of living of the vast majority. In most of Asia and Eastern Europe, which had more capital-intensive farming systems and hierarchical societies, the average incomes were only $500–$700. Most people lived at subsistence, and the surplus was extracted by the state, the aristocracy, and the rich merchants. Northwestern Europe and the USA had incomes four to six times subsistence. Only in these societies did workers live above bare-bones subsistence, as Figure 3 shows. These economies were sufficiently productive to also support aristocracies and merchants.

Bare-bones subsistence has further implications for social wellbeing and economic progress. First, people living on the bare-bones diet are short. The average height of Italians who enlisted in the Habsburg army fell from 167 cm to 162 cm as their diet shifted from bread to polenta. In contrast, English soldiers in the 18th century averaged 172 cm due to their better nutrition. (Today, the average man is 176–8 cm tall in the USA, UK, and Italy, while the Dutch are 184 cm tall.) When people's heights are stunted for lack of food, their life expectation is also cut, and their health in general declines. Second, people living at subsistence are less well educated. Sir Frederick Eden, who surveyed labourers' incomes and spending patterns in England in the 1790s, described a London gardener who spent 6 pence per week sending two of his children to school. The family bought wheat bread, meat, beer, sugar, and tea, and his earnings (£37.75 per year) were about four times subsistence (just under £10). If their income were suddenly cut to subsistence, vast economies would have had to be made, and who can doubt that the children would have been removed from school? High wages contributed to economic growth by sustaining good health and supporting widespread education. Finally, and most paradoxically, bare-bones subsistence removes the economic motivation for a country to develop economically. The need for more output from a day's work is great, but labour is so cheap that businesses have no incentive to invent or adopt machinery to raise productivity. Bare-bones subsistence is a poverty trap. The Industrial Revolution was the result of high wages – and not just their cause.

Chapter 2
The rise of the West

Why has the world become increasingly unequal? Both 'fundamentals' like geography, institutions, or culture and 'accidents of history' played a role.

Geography is important. Malaria holds back the tropics, and Britain's coal deposits underpinned the Industrial Revolution. Geography is rarely the whole explanation, however, for its significance depends on technology and economic opportunities; indeed, one of the aims of technology is to reduce the burden of bad geography. In the 18th century, for instance, the location of coal and iron deposits determined the location of blast furnaces. Today, ocean transportation is so cheap that Japan and Korea obtain their coal and iron ore from Australia and Brazil.

Culture has been a popular explanation for economic success. Max Weber, for instance, contended that Protestantism made northern Europeans more rational and hard-working than anyone else. Weber's theory looked plausible in 1905 when Protestant Britain was richer than Catholic Italy. Today, however, the reverse is true, and Weber's theory is no longer tenable. Another cultural argument claims that peasant farmers in the Third World are poor because they cling to traditional methods and fail to respond to economic incentives. The contrary, however, is true: farmers in poor countries experiment with new crops and methods, employ labour to the degree that it pays, adopt modern fertilizers and seeds when they are cost-effective, and shift their cropping in response to price changes like farmers in the rich countries. Peasants are poor because they receive low prices for their crops and because they lack appropriate technology – not because they refuse to use it.

While cultural explanations that invoke irrationality and laziness are suspect, there are aspects of culture that affect economic performance. In particular, widespread literacy and numeracy have been necessary (if not sufficient) conditions for economic success since the 17th century. These mental skills help trade to flourish and science and technology to develop. Literacy and numeracy are spread by mass education, which has become a universal strategy for economic development.

The importance of political and legal institutions is hotly debated. Many economists argue that economic success is the result of secure property rights, low taxes, and minimal government. Arbitrary government is bad for growth because it leads to high taxes, regulations, corruption, and rent-seeking – all of which reduce the incentive to produce. These views are applied historically by arguing that absolutist monarchies such as Spain and France or empires like those of China, Rome, or the Aztecs stifled economic activity by prohibiting international trade, threatening property or, indeed, life itself. These views, of course, echo those of Adam Smith and other 18th-century liberals. Successful economic development was due to the replacement of absolutism with representative government. The Netherlands revolted against Spanish rule in 1568 and organized itself as a republic. The country grew rapidly afterwards. The English economy suffered in the early 17th century under the rules of James I and Charles I, who imposed taxes of disputed legality and levied forced loans. Charles's attempts to rule without Parliament failed, civil war broke out, and, in 1649, the

King was convicted of treason and executed. After the Restoration, disputes between Crown and Parliament continued, however, finally culminating in the Glorious Revolution of 1688 when James II fled the country and Parliament gave the Crown to William and Mary. With Parliament supreme, absolutism was checked, and the economy boomed. So goes the economists' history.

However, as economists have been celebrating the superiority of English institutions, historians have been investigating how absolutist monarchy and Oriental despotism actually worked. The usual finding is that they promoted peace, order, and good government. Trade flourished as a result, regional specialization increased, and cities expanded. As regions became more specialized, the national income rose in a process that has come to be called 'Smithian growth'. The greatest threat to prosperity was invasion by barbarians attracted to the civilization's wealth – not expropriation or intervention by the emperor.

The first globalization

While institutions, culture, and geography always lurk in the background, technological change, globalization, and economic policy turn out to have been the immediate causes of unequal development. The Industrial Revolution itself, moreover, was the result of the first phase of globalization that began in the late 15th century with the voyages of Columbus, Magellan, and the other great explorers. The great divergence, therefore, begins with the first globalization.

Globalization required ships that could sail the high seas. Europeans did not have them until the 15th century. These newly invented 'full-rigged' ships had three masts – the front and middle were square-rigged and the aft was lateen-rigged. Sturdier hulls and the use of rudders instead of steering oars made ships that could navigate the globe.

Initially, the commercial impact of the full-rigged ship was felt in Europe. In the 15th century, the Dutch began shipping Polish grain from Danzig to the Netherlands and, by the late 16th century, to Spain, Portugal, and the Mediterranean. Textiles quickly followed. Italian cities had dominated the cloth industry in the Middle Ages, but English and Dutch producers contrived to make lightweight worsted cloth in imitation of Italian fabrics. By the early 17th century, the Mediterranean was flooded with these 'new draperies', and the English and Dutch drove the Italians out of business. This was a momentous change and began the relocation of Europe's manufacturing industry to northwestern Europe.

The most dramatic impact of the full-rigged ship, however, was in the Voyages of Discovery. Networks of Indian, Arab, and Venetian merchants shipped pepper and spices from Asia, across the Middle East, to Europe, and the Portuguese hoped to out-compete them with an all-water route. In the 15th century, the Portuguese sailed south along the African coast in search of a sea route to the East.

In 1498, Vasco da Gama reached Cochin in India, and filled his ship with pepper. The price in Cochin was about 4% of the price in Europe (Figure 5). The other 96% of the price difference was transport costs. By 1760, the gap between the Indian and English prices in Figure 5 had dropped by 85%, and that reduction is a measure of the efficiency gain from the all-sea route. In the 16th century, however, only Portugal benefited from the cut in transport costs since its state trading company kept the price at the medieval level and pocketed the savings as profits. It was the arrival of the English and Dutch East Indies companies in the early 17th century that broke Portugal's maritime monopoly and cut the European price by two-thirds. The real price received by Indian sellers increased by only a small amount: most of the efficiency gains from the Asian trade were reaped by European consumers.

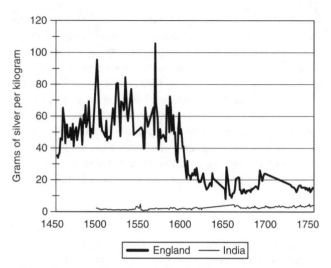

5. Price of pepper, adjusted to price level of 1600

The Genoese sailor Christopher Columbus, of course, proposed the alternative of sailing west from Europe directly to Asia. He talked King Ferdinand and Queen Isabella of Spain into financing his expedition and landed in the Bahamas on 12 October 1492, convinced that he had reached the East Indies. But it was the Americas he had 'discovered', and that changed the history of the world.

Columbus's and da Gama's voyages set off a scramble for empire, and the Portuguese and Spanish were the early winners. In the two battles of Diu (1509 and 1538), the Portuguese defeated Venetian, Ottoman, and Asian forces and established their hegemony in the Indian Ocean. Then they pushed east towards Indonesia, establishing a string of colonies along the way. Eventually, the Portuguese reached the fabled Spice Islands (that is, the Moluccas in Indonesia), where nutmeg, cloves, and mace were indigenous. The Portuguese also accidentally discovered Brazil in 1500, which became their biggest colony.

Spain's empire was even richer. The greatest successes were the conquests of the Aztec Empire in 1521 by Hernán Cortés and the Inca Empire 11 years later by Francisco Pizarro. In both cases, small Spanish forces defeated large native armies through a combination of firearms, horses, guile, and smallpox. Looting the Aztecs and the Incas brought immediate wealth to Spain. Conquest was followed by the discovery of large silver deposits in Bolivia and Mexico. The silver flooding into Spain paid for the Habsburg armies fighting the Protestants across Europe, provided Europeans with the cash to buy up Asian goods, and unleashed decades of inflation known as the Price Revolution.

The imperial exploits of northern Europeans were modest in the 16th century. The English sent Giovanni Caboto (John Cabot) west in 1497, and he made it to Cape Breton, or Newfoundland. This counted as discovery, although Basque sailors had been fishing the Grand Banks for centuries. The French sent Jacques Cartier to Canada on three voyages in the 1530s and 1540s. Fur trading with the natives counted for little compared to Mexico or the Moluccas.

It was not until the 17th century that the northern Europeans became important imperialists. Their favourite organization was an East Indies company that combined imperialism with private enterprise. Typically, these firms were highly capitalized joint stock companies that traded in Asia or the Americas, maintained military and naval forces, and established fortified trading posts abroad. All of the northern powers had them. The English East India Company was chartered in 1600 and its Dutch counterpart two years later.

The Dutch East Indies Company created a Dutch Empire in Asia at the expense of the Portuguese. The Dutch seized the Moluccas in 1605, Malacca in 1641, Ceylon in 1658, and Cochin in 1662. They made Jakarta the capital of their Indonesian possessions in 1619. The Dutch also seized Brazil in the 1630s and 1640s. They colonized sugar islands in the Caribbean, and founded New York in 1624 and the Cape Colony in South Africa in 1652.

The English also created an empire in the 17th century. In Asia, the English East India Company defeated the Portuguese in the naval battle of Swally off Surat in 1612. Subsequently, fortified trading posts were established at Surat (1612), Madras (1639), Bombay (1668), and Calcutta (1690). By 1647, the East India Company had 23 establishments in India. In the Americas, a variety of individuals and groups established colonies. Jamestown, Virginia, was the first success, in 1607. The legendary Plymouth colony followed in 1620, and the much more important Massachusetts Bay colony ten years later. The Bahamas and a string of islands were taken in the Caribbean in the 1620s and 1630s. Jamaica was added in 1655.

The English state actively expanded its empire – particularly at the expense of the Dutch. The first steps were taken by Oliver Cromwell, during the Commonwealth (1640–60), and continued after the Restoration. Expenditure on the navy was greatly increased. The first Navigation Act was passed in 1651. This mercantilist measure was intended to exclude the Dutch from trading with the English empire. The first Anglo-Dutch War (1652–4) was fought for commercial advantage, but was far from successful. After the Restoration of Charles II in 1660, the Navigation Acts were reinstated and extended, the (now Royal) Navy was expanded, and more wars were fought against the Dutch in 1665–7 and 1672–4. New York was seized in 1664. English colonies were established along the American coast from Georgia to Maine. Their economies grew rapidly by exporting tobacco, rice, wheat, and meat to England and the Caribbean. By 1770, the population of British America had reached 2.8 million, or almost half of England's.

English and Dutch trade with their colonies drove their economies forward. Cities and export-oriented manufacturing grew. The

Table 3. Percentage distribution of the population by sector, 1500–1750

| | 1500 | | | 1750 | | |
	urban	rural nonagri- culture	agri- culture	urban	rural nonagri- culture	agri- culture
greatest transformation						
England	7%	18%	74%	23%	32%	45%
significant modernization						
Netherlands	30	14	56	36	22	42
Belgium	28	14	58	22	27	51
slight evolution						
Germany	8	18	73	9	27	64
France	9	18	73	13	26	61

(continued)

| | 1500 rural | | | 1750 rural | | |
	urban	nonagri-culture	agri-culture	urban	nonagri-culture	agri-culture
Austria/Hungary	5	19	76	78	32	61
Poland	6	19	75	4	36	60
little change						
Italy	22	16	62	22	19	59
Spain	19	16	65	21	17	62

occupational structure changed accordingly. Table 3 divides the populations of the main European countries into three groups: agricultural, urban, and rural non-agricultural. In the Middle Ages, about three-quarters of the population was engaged in farming, most manufacturing was carried out in cities, and the 'rural non-agricultural population' consisted of village craftsmen, priests, carters, and the servants of country houses. In 1500, Italy and Spain were the most advanced economies, with the largest cities that produced the best manufactures. The Low Countries (principally modern-day Belgium) were an extension of this economy. The Dutch population was very small, and England was little more than a sheep walk.

By the eve of the Industrial Revolution, there had been far-reaching changes. England was the most transformed country. The fraction of the population in agriculture had dropped to 45%. England was the most rapidly urbanizing country in Europe. London grew from 50,000 in 1500 to 200,000 in 1600 to 500,000 in 1700 and, finally, to one million in 1800. The 'rural non-agricultural share' of the population was 32% in 1750. Most of these people were engaged in manufacturing industries, and their products were shipped across Europe and, sometimes, around the world. Artisans in Witney, Oxfordshire, for instance, sold blankets to the Hudson Bay Company, which swapped them for fur with the natives of Canada. The economy of the Low Countries developed along similar lines. The Netherlands were even more urbanized than England and also had large, export-oriented rural industries.

The rest of Europe was much less transformed. The great continental countries saw a small reduction in the share of their populations in agriculture and a corresponding increase in rural industry with little extra urbanization. Spain and Italy look stationary, with no change in the distribution of their populations.

Spain was particularly unlucky. In the 16th century, it looked like the most successful imperialist, for Latin America yielded so much silver. Silver imports, however, led to much greater inflation in Spain than elsewhere. As a result, Spanish agriculture and manufacturing became uncompetitive. The constancy in the share of the urban population in Spain masks great changes – the populations of old industrial cities collapsed while Madrid expanded on the basis of American loot. Globalization spurred northwestern Europe forward but held southern Europe back.

Success in the global economy had major implications for economic development, including:

First, the growth in urbanization and rural manufacturing increased the demand for labour and led to tight labour markets and high wages. Living standards were high in London and Amsterdam (Figure 3).

Second, growing cities and a high-wage economy put great demands on agriculture for food and labour. The result was agricultural revolutions in both England and the Netherlands. Output per farm worker increased by about 50% in both countries and reached the highest levels in Europe.

Third, growing urban demand also led to energy revolutions in both England and the Netherlands. In the Middle Ages, charcoal and firewood were the principal fuels burned in cities. As the cities grew, wood prices skyrocketed, and substitute fuels were developed. In the Netherlands, the alternative was peat; in England, it was coal. Coal was mined in Durham and Northumberland and shipped down the coast to London. England was the only country in the world with a large coal-mining industry in the 18th century, and that also gave it access to the cheapest energy in the world, as Figure 6 indicates.

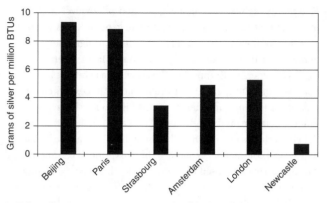

6. Price of energy

Table 4. Adult literacy, 1500 and 1800. Percentage of the adult population that could sign its name

	1500	1800
England	6	53
Netherlands	10	68
Belgium	10	49
Germany	6	35
France	7	37
Austria/Hungary	6	21
Poland	6	21
Italy	9	22
Spain	9	20

Fourth, the high-wage economy generated a high level of literacy, numeracy, and skill formation in general. Table 4 shows estimates of literacy (measured by the ability to sign one's name rather than make a mark) in 1500 and 1800. Literacy rose everywhere in Europe, but the growth was greatest in northwestern Europe. The Reformation does not explain the rise, as is often assumed, for literacy was as high in northeastern France, Belgium, and the Rhine Valley – all Catholic areas – as in the Netherlands or England. The rise in literacy was due to the high-wage, commercial economy. The expansion of commerce and manufacturing increased the demand for education by making it economically valuable; at the same time, the high-wage economy provided parents with the money to pay for schooling their children.

Chapter 3
The Industrial Revolution

The Industrial Revolution (roughly 1760 to 1850) was a turning point in world history, for it inaugurated the era of sustained economic growth. The Revolution was not the abrupt discontinuity that its name suggests but was the result of the transformations of the early modern economy discussed in the last chapter. The rate of economic growth achieved in the century after 1760 (1.5% per year) was very low by the standards of recent growth miracles in which GDP has grown by as much as 8–10% per year. However, Britain was continuously extending the world's technology frontier, and that is always slower going than catching up to the leader by importing its technology, which is how countries have grown very rapidly. Moreover, the great achievement of the British Industrial Revolution was that it led to continuous growth, so that income compounded to the mass prosperity of today.

Technological change was the motor of the Industrial Revolution. There were famous inventions like the steam engine, the machines to spin and weave cotton, and the new processes to smelt and refine iron and steel using coal instead of wood fuels. In addition, there were a host of simpler machines that raised labour productivity in unglamorous industries like hats, pins, and nails. There was also a range of new English products, many of which, like Wedgwood porcelain, were inspired by Asian manufactures.

In the 19th century, engineers extended the 18th-century mechanical inventions across the board. The steam engine was applied to transportation with the invention of the railway and the steamship. Power-driven machinery, whose use was initially restricted to textile mills, was applied to industry generally.

The question is: why was the revolutionary technology invented in England rather than the Netherlands or France or, for that matter, China or India?

Cultural and political context

The Industrial Revolution took place in a particular political and cultural context that was favourable to innovation, and that may help to explain it.

The English constitution has been a model for European liberals and modern economists alike. It was far from democratic: only 3–5% of the English could vote and even fewer of the Scots. Much power remained with the Crown – in particular, the power to make war and peace. While Parliament had a constitutional right to refuse funds for war, it never did.

The English constitution had many features that promoted economic growth, although they were not the ones stressed by modern economists, who emphasize restrictions on taxation and the security of property. Parliamentary supremacy actually resulted in the reverse. While French monarchs claimed to be absolute, they could not increase taxes without consent, and it was a crisis in public finances that precipitated the Revolution by forcing Louis XVI to convene the États généraux in 1789. The nobility in France were exempt from taxation, but the English Parliament introduced a land tax in 1693 that was imposed on peers as well as commoners. Most tax revenue, however, was raised from excise duties on consumer goods like beer and imports like sugar and tobacco. These taxes were borne primarily by workers, who were not represented in Parliament. Parliament may have checked the Crown, but, in the absence of democracy, who checked Parliament?

In the event, the English state collected about twice as much per person as the French state and spent a larger fraction of the national income. It is arguable that these expenditures promoted economic growth. Most of the money was spent on the army and the navy. The former was occasionally directed abroad but was always available to maintain domestic order by suppressing assemblies opposed to machinery or in favour of democracy. The navy was directed to expand Britain's empire and promote the country's commerce. Even the workers gained from this since imperialism was the basis of the high-wage economy, which in turn led to growth by inducing labour-saving technical change. Had Louis XIV had the power to levy taxes, he might have advanced French prosperity by maintaining the French navy in a permanent state of readiness rather than enlarging or contracting it in response to the swing between war and peace.

Growth was also promoted by Parliament's power to take people's property against their wishes. This was not possible in France. Indeed, one could argue that France suffered because property was too secure: profitable irrigation projects were not undertaken in Provence because France had no counterpart to the private acts of the British Parliament that overrode property owners opposed to the enclosure of their land or the construction of canals or turnpikes across it. What the Glorious Revolution meant in practice was that the 'despotic power' of the state that 'was only available intermittently before 1688...was always available thereafter'.

In addition to a favourable political system, the Industrial Revolution was sustained by the emerging scientific culture. The Scientific Revolution of the 17th century led to a handful of discoveries about the natural world that were applied by inventors in the 18th. In addition, the success of natural philosophy lent credibility to the scientific method, that is, the view that the world is governed by laws that can be discovered by observation and applied to the improvement of human life. Newton's model of the Solar System was the greatest achievement, and it inspired a reorientation of upper-class ideas about religion and nature.

How much popular culture shared in this reorientation is an open question. There are important examples of working-class inventors adopting the Newtonian model. John Harrison, for instance, was lent a copy of Saunderson's lectures on natural philosophy, a Newtonian tract, by a clergyman, and made a copy of it. Did this early interest in Newton dispose Harrison to invent the chronometer? On the other hand, there was continued popular enthusiasm for witchcraft, which was the medieval alternative to science. It is likely that more people believed in witchcraft than in Newton's laws of motion. John Wesley's preaching was attracting millions of followers, and he was of the view that the 'giving up of witchcraft is, in effect, giving up the Bible'.

Popular culture was more directly transformed by social changes than by Newton's *Principia Mathematica*. The most powerful changes were urbanization and the growth of commerce. They encouraged the spread of literacy and numeracy by increasing their value. By the 18th century, most sons of craftsmen, artisans, shop keepers, and farmers, and a smaller share of the sons of labourers, received several years of primary education. Many girls were also schooled. The result was a public that read newspapers and followed politics to an unprecedented degree. It was a new world when a radical like Tom Paine could achieve celebrity by selling hundreds of thousands of copies of *The Rights of Man*.

Explaining the Industrial Revolution

Scientific discoveries were known across Europe, and upper-class enthusiasm for natural philosophy was universal. These cultural developments, therefore, cannot explain why the Industrial

Revolution was British. Instead, the explanation lies in Britain's unique structure of wages and prices. Britain's high-wage, cheap-energy economy made it profitable for British firms to invent and use the breakthrough technologies of the Industrial Revolution.

In Chapters 1 and 2, we saw that wages in Britain were sufficiently high for most people to eat bread, beef, and beer, instead of subsisting on oatmeal. More to the point, so far as technology is concerned, British wages were high relative to the price of capital (Figure 7). In the late 1500s, the wage rate relative to the price of capital services was similar in southern England, France, and Austria, which are representative of continental Europe. By the middle of the 18th century, however, labour relative to capital was 60% more expensive in England than on the continent. In the early 19th century, which is the first time a comparison can be made with Asia, labour was even cheaper relative to capital in India than it was in France or Austria. The incentive to mechanize production was correspondingly less in India.

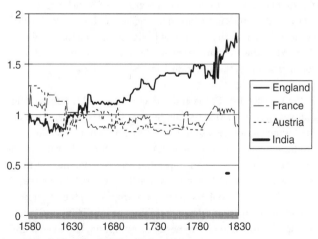

7. **Wage relative to price of capital services**

It was the same story with energy. Britain, especially on the coal fields in the north and in the midlands, had the cheapest energy in the world. Consequently, energy was much cheaper compared to labour in Britain than it was anywhere else.

As a result of these differences in wages and prices, businesses in England found it profitable to use technology that saved on expensive labour by increasing the use of cheap energy and capital. With more capital and energy at their disposal, British workers became more productive – the secret of economic growth. In Asia and Africa, the cheapness of labour led to the opposite result.

The cotton industry

Eric Hobsbawm famously wrote: 'Whoever says Industrial Revolution says Cotton.' From tiny beginnings in the mid-18th century, the industry grew to be Britain's largest, accounting for 8% of GDP in 1830 and 16% of British manufacturing jobs. Cotton was the first industry to be transformed by factory production. The growth of cotton led to the explosive growth of Manchester and many smaller cities in the north of England and Scotland. Britain's expansion came at the expense of India, China, and the Middle East. When these countries eventually began to re-industrialize, cotton was one of the first industries they turned to.

In the 17th century, China and India had the world's largest cotton industries. Bengal, Madras, and Surat shipped cotton cloth across the Indian Ocean and as far as West Africa. Cotton was also produced in small centres across Asia and Africa. The various East Indies companies began to ship cotton calicoes and muslins to Europe in the late 17th century where they successfully competed against linen and wool, the principal European textiles. Cotton was so successful that France prohibited its import in 1686, and the English restricted its domestic consumption. However, there was a large export market in West Africa, where cotton cloth was bartered for slaves. In this market, English cloth competed against Indian cloth.

International competition was the spur that led to the mechanization of cotton spinning. The finer the cotton, the more time it took to spin. Wages were so high in England that competition with India was only possible in the coarsest fabrics. There was a large market in finer fabrics, but England could only compete if machines were invented to reduce labour. The stakes were considerable: in 1750, Bengal spun about 85 million pounds of cotton per year, while Britain managed only 3 million. There were numerous attempts to mechanize production. James Hargreaves' spinning jenny, developed in the mid-1760s, was the first commercially successful machine, followed closely by Richard Arkwright's water frame. Samuel Crompton's mule, invented in the 1770s, married the jenny and the water frame (hence its name) and became the basis of mechanical spinning for a century.

These machines owed nothing to scientific discoveries. None involved great conceptual leaps; instead, they required years of experimental engineering to come up with designs that worked reliably. Thomas Edison's remark that 'invention is 1% inspiration and 99% perspiration' is on the mark for the cotton industry.

The crux in explaining why the Industrial Revolution was invented in Britain is, therefore, explaining why British inventors spent so much time and money doing R&D (Research and Development, that is, Edison's 'perspiration') to operationalize what were often banal ideas. The key is that the machines they invented increased the use of capital to save labour. Consequently, they were profitable to use where labour was expensive and capital was cheap, that is, in England. Nowhere else were the machines profitable. That is why the Industrial Revolution was British.

Cotton yarn was manufactured in three stages. First, the bales of raw cotton were broken open and the dirt and debris removed.

Second, the cotton was carded, that is, the strands of cotton were aligned into a loose strand called a roving by dragging the cotton between cards studded with pins. Third, the roving was spun into yarn. Before machines, the whorl and drop spindle was used to make fine yarn, while the spinning wheel made coarse yarn. In each case, the roving was stretched to thin it, then twisted to strengthen it, and, finally, the yarn was wound on a spindle to send to weavers.

All of these stages were mechanized, and, indeed, Richard Arkwright's greatest achievement was to design a mill (Cromford Mill No.2) in which machines were laid out in a logical sequence, and which became the model for the early cotton mills in Britain, the USA, and the continent. Spinning was the crux of the problem, and inventors had worked on it since at least the 1730s. Lewis Paul and John Wyatt were on the right track in the 1740s and 1750s with their system of roller spinning, but their mill in Birmingham always lost money. James Hargreaves' spinning jenny, invented in the 1760s, was the first commercially successful spinning machine. It elaborated the spinning wheel by running many spindles off one wheel and using draw bars and linkages to mimic the movements of the spinner's hands. Arkwright employed clockmakers for five years in order to perfect his water frame that used rollers. With roller spinning, the roving was stretched by pulling it through successive pairs of rollers, which, like mangles, dragged the cotton forward. Each pair of rollers moved faster than the previous, so they lengthened and thinned the yarn by pulling against each other.

Crompton's mule was the last great spinning machine. It combined the draw bars of Hargreaves' jenny with the rollers of Arkwright's water frame to make a machine that could spin yarn far finer than any of the other machines. The jenny and the water frame made England competitive with Indian producers in coarse yarn; the mule made England the low-cost producer in fine yarn as well.

The economics of these machines were similar. All of them reduced the hours of labour needed to produce one pound of yarn. At the same time, they increased the capital required per pound. As a result, the cost saving from mechanical spinning was higher where labour was more expensive. In the 1780s, the rate of return to building an Arkwright mill was 40% in England, 9% in France, and less than 1% in India. With investors expecting a 15% return on fixed capital, it is no surprise that about 150 Arkwright mills were erected in Britain in the 1780s, 4 in France, and none in India. Relative profitability was similar with the spinning jenny, as was the result – 20,000 jennies were installed in England on the eve of the French Revolution, 900 in France, and none in India. There was no point in spending much time or money to invent mechanical spinning in France or India since it was not profitable to use it there.

The situation did not remain like this, which is why the Industrial Revolution spread to other countries. Arkwright's mills created an integrated series of machines that cut costs by more than Hargreaves' jenny. Crompton's mule cut the cost of spinning fine yarn. A long list of inventors improved the mule over the next half century. They economized on capital as well as on labour. By the 1820s, improved cotton machinery could be profitably installed on the continent, and by the 1850s, it proved profitable to install even more improved machinery in low-wage economies such as Mexico and India. By the 1870s, factory cotton production began to shift into the Third World.

The steam engine

The steam engine was the most transformative technology of the Industrial Revolution since it allowed mechanical power to be used in a wide range of industries as well as in railways and ocean ships.

Steam power was a spin-off of the Scientific Revolution. Atmospheric pressure was one of the hot topics of 17th-century physics. It was investigated by famous scientists across Europe, including Galileo, Torricelli, von Guericke, Huygens, and Boyle. By the middle of the century, Huygens and von Guericke had shown that, if a vacuum was created in a cylinder, then the pressure of the atmosphere would force a piston into it. In 1675, the Frenchman Denis Papin used this idea to make a crude, proto steam engine. A practical engine was completed by Thomas Newcomen in 1712 in Dudley, after 12 years of experimentation. Newcomen's engine involved boiling water to make steam, filling a cylinder with it, and then injecting cold water into the cylinder to condense the steam so that the pressure of the atmosphere depressed a piston into the cylinder. The piston was connected to a rocker beam that raised a pump as the piston was depressed.

The steam engine emphasizes the importance of economic incentives in inducing invention. The science of the engine was pan-European, but the R&D was conducted in England because that was where it paid to use the steam engine. The purpose of the Newcomen engine was to drain mines, and Britain had many more mines than any other country due to the large coal industry. In addition, the early steam engines burned vast quantities of coal, so they were cost-effective only where energy was cheap. John Theophilus Desaguliers wrote in the 1730s that the Newcomen engines were 'now of general use ... in the Coal-Works, where the Power of the Fire is made from the Refuse of the Coals, which would not otherwise be sold'. They were scarcely used anywhere else. Despite the scientific breakthroughs, the steam engine would not have been developed had the British coal industry not existed.

Steam power became a technology that could be applied to many purposes and used around the world, but only after the engine was improved. This was not accomplished before the 1840s. Engineers like John Smeaton, James Watt, Richard Trevithick, and Arthur Woolf studied and modified the engine, reducing its energy requirements and smoothing its delivery of power. Coal consumption per horse power-hour of power was cut from 44 pounds in the Newcomen engines of the 1730s to one pound in the triple expansion marine engines of the late 19th century. The genius of British engineering undid the country's competitive advantage by improving its technology to the point that it could be profitably used around the globe. This allowed the Industrial Revolution to spread abroad and the whole world to industrialize.

Continuing invention

The greatest achievement of the Industrial Revolution was that the 18th-century inventions were not one-offs like the achievements of earlier centuries. Instead, the 18th-century inventions kicked off a continuing stream of innovations.

Cotton continued to be a focus of effort. While the 18th-century inventions had turned spinning into a factory system, weaving was still done on hand looms in cottages. This was changed by the Reverend Edmund Cartwright, who spent decades and wasted his fortune perfecting a power loom. He was inspired by automatons like Jacques de Vaucanson's mechanical duck that wowed the court in Versailles by flapping, eating, and defecating! (Voltaire quipped: 'Without Vaucanson's duck, you have nothing to remind you of the glory of France.') If a mechanism could poop like that, couldn't it also do useful work? Cartwright thought so and patented his first loom in 1785 and an improved version in 1792. It was not commercially viable, however. Many inventors improved it piecemeal. By the 1820s, the power loom was displacing hand looms in England, but they continued in use until the 1850s. The power loom greatly increased capital costs while reducing labour costs, so its adoption was sensitive to factor prices as well as the relative efficiency of the two methods. It is singularly important that the power loom was taken up more rapidly in the USA than it was in Britain. By the 1820s, wages were already higher in the USA, and the pattern of technological innovation reflected that difference.

Cotton also led the way in the application of steam power to factories. Experiments had been made earlier, of course. In 1784, Boulton and Watt invested in the Albion Flour Mill, the first large-scale steam-powered factory, to promote their engines. The next year, steam was applied to a cotton mill for the first time. However, most factories were driven by water power until the 1840s. It was only then that the fuel consumption of steam engines had dropped sufficiently to make them a cheaper source of power. After that, the use of steam to power industry expanded continuously.

Steam power also revolutionized transportation in the 19th century. Everyone who invented a high-pressure steam engine (Cugnot, Trevithick, Evans) used it to power a land vehicle, but they were all unsuccessful since they could not negotiate the unpaved roads. One solution was to put the engine on rails. Coal and ore had long been hauled in carts rolling on primitive wooden rails laid in mines. In the 18th century, iron rails replaced wood, and the lines were extended. In 1804, Richard Trevithick built the first steam locomotive for a railway at the Penydarren Ironworks in Wales. From then on, colliery railways became the testing ground for steam locomotives. The 26-mile Stockton and Darlington Railway (1825) was planned as a coal railway but showed there was money to be made in carrying general freight and passengers. The first general-purpose railway was the 35-mile Liverpool and Manchester Line, opened in 1830. It was a great success and set off a frenzy of railway promotion in Britain. Almost 10,000 kilometres of track were open by 1850, and 30 years later, the network reached 25,000 kilometres.

Steam power was also applied to water travel – another way of avoiding bad roads! Invention was international from the start. The first working vessels were French – the *Palmipède* (1774) and *Pyroscaphe* (1783) – and the first commercially successful ship was Robert Fulton's *Clermont*, which plied the Hudson River from

1807. Two years later, John Molson, the Canadian brewer, sailed steamships on the St Lawrence River using engines built in Trois-Rivière, Québec.

By the middle of the 19th century, steam was displacing sail in ocean transportation. Britain became the centre of world shipbuilding in view of its pre-eminence in iron and engineering. Brunel's *Great Western* (1838) marked a breakthrough, for it established that a ship could carry enough coal to cross the Atlantic, and his *Great Britain* (1843) was the first ship to be built of iron and to use a propeller instead of paddle wheels. It took another half century, however, for steam to vanquish sail. The reason was that ships still had to carry their own coal, so they lost much of their cargo space on long voyages. The first routes to shift to steam were consequently short. As the coal requirements of steam engines were reduced, ships could sail longer distances with the same amount of coal, and the distance for which steam could undercut sail lengthened. The last routes to fall were those from China to Britain where clipper ships survived until the end of the 19th century.

Steam power is an example of a general-purpose technology (GPT), that is a technology that can be applied to a variety of uses. Other GPTs include electricity and computers. It takes decades to develop the potential of GPTs, so their contribution to economic growth takes place long after their invention. That was certainly true for steam. As late as 1800, almost a century after Newcomen's invention, steam power made only a minute contribution to the British economy. By the middle of the 19th century, however, the potential of steam was finally being realized as it was applied widely to transportation and industry. Half of the growth of labour productivity in Britain in the mid-19th century was due to steam. This long-run pay-off is an important reason that economic growth continued through the century. Another reason was the growing application of science to industry, which we will consider in the next chapter.

Chapter 4
The ascent of the rich

Between 1815 and 1870, the Industrial Revolution spread from Britain to the continent with remarkable success. Not only did the West European countries catch up to the leader, but they joined the leader in forming a group of innovators that has jointly advanced the world's technology frontier ever since. Of course, North America also industrialized in the 19th century and soon joined the innovation club. The USA, indeed, has become the world's technological leader, but its performance should be thought of as 'first among equals' – the latter including the West Europeans and the British.

Whether Western Europe's success is a surprise depends on one's view of the Industrial Revolution. Some historians think that the Revolution was as likely to have happened in France or Germany as in Britain and that the big problem, therefore, is explaining why it occurred in Europe rather than Asia. For them, it is obvious that the continent would quickly industrialize. Other historians, however, think that there were fundamental differences in institutions or incentives between Britain and the continent, in which case, the industrialization of Western Europe requires an explanation.

Institutionalists believe that continental development in the 18th century was held back by archaic institutions. These were swept away by the French Revolution, which was exported to most of Europe by the armies of the Republic and Napoleon. Everywhere the French conquered, they remodelled Europe in their new image, which included the abolition of serfdom, equality before the law, a new legal regime (the *Code Napoléon*), the expropriation of monastic property, the creation of national markets by the abolition of internal tariffs and erection of a common external tariff, a rationalized tax system, universal secular primary education and the extension of modern secondary schools, technical institutes and universities, the promotion of scientific societies and culture. Countries like Prussia that were defeated by Napoleon but not incorporated into his empire also modernized their institutions. Napoleon's wars prevented these reforms from having immediate effect, but, after Waterloo, Europe was ripe for industrial take-off.

Another line of explanation emphasizes the incentives to adopt the new industrial technology. First, Britain's early start meant that British manufacturers could out-compete those on the continent, and, second, the technology of the Industrial Revolution was inappropriate for continental countries where wages were lower and energy prices generally higher than in Britain. Continental industrialization required the invention of appropriate technology and protection from British competition while that took place.

While Britain did not have a policy to 'industrialize', most countries since have had a strategy to emulate its success. In the 19th century, a package of development policies emerged that many countries followed. These policies were originally worked out in the USA (see Chapter 6) and then promoted in Europe by Friedrich List, a German who lived in the USA from 1825 to 1832 and then returned to Germany to write *The National System of Political Economy* (1841). The standard development strategy, which built on Napoleon's institutional revolution, had four imperatives: create a large national market by abolishing internal tariffs and improving transportation; erect an external tariff to protect 'infant industries' from British competition; create banks to stabilize the currency and provide business with capital; and, finally, establish mass education to speed the adoption and invention of technology. This development strategy helped continental Europe to catch up to Britain.

Germany is a good example. In the Middle Ages, it was divided into hundreds of independent political units. The number was whittled down to 38 at the Congress of Vienna in 1815. Prussia, which was the largest German state, instituted universal primary education in the 18th century. Other states followed. By the middle of the 19th century, primary education was close to universal across Germany.

Prussia also took the lead in creating a national market by forming the *Zollverein* (customs union) in 1818 to unify its territory. Other German states gradually joined. The *Zollverein* both abolished internal traffics and created a common external tariff to keep out British manufactures. The economic union formed the basis of the German Empire created in 1871.

The integration of markets was reinforced by building railways. The first German railway (6 kilometres long) was built from Nuremberg to Fürth in 1835, just five years after the Liverpool to Manchester Railway. Mainline railways were laid out in the 1850s and branch lines in the next decades. About 63,000 kilometres were open in 1913.

Investment banks, which played no role in British industrialization, were prominent on the continent. The earliest experiment was the *Société Générale pour favoriser l'Industrie Nationale des Pays-Bas* founded in 1822 to promote industrial development in the Low Countries. German private banks began to do the same thing. The *Crédit Mobilier*, established in France in 1852 to finance railways and industry, was a giant step forward.

The following year, it spun off the Bank of Darmstadt, which popularized the joint-stock investment bank in Germany. By 1872, all of the giant German banks (Commerzbank, Dresdner, Deutsche, etc.) were founded. They had many branches to assemble the capital of many depositors. They formed lasting relationships with industrial clients, providing them with long-term funds as current account overdrafts at low rates of interest. Often these loans were secured with mortgages on industrial property, and bank representatives served as directors of the industrial firms. These banks financed the great expansion of German industry between 1880 and the First World War.

Between 1815 and 1870, all of the major industries of the Industrial Revolution were established on the continent on a profitable basis. Spinning jennies and early Arkwright mills had not been profitable in France before the Revolution, but subsequent technical progress cut the cost of producing coarse yarn by 42% by the mid-1830s. These cost declines made the new-style mills profitable to erect. By 1840, France was spinning 54,000 tons of cotton per year, compared to Britain's 192,000. Production had begun in Germany (11,000 tons) and Belgium (7,000). It is worth noting that the USA at this time was already processing 47,000 tons of raw cotton.

A modern iron industry was also established on the continent by 1870. Charcoal was the fuel used to smelt and purify iron before the 18th century. Charcoal was replaced by coke, a refined form of coal, in one of the most famous innovations of the Industrial Revolution. This technique was put into practice by Abraham Darby at the Coalbrookdale Iron Company in 1709. Coke iron, however, was not cost-effective in the manufacture of rolled iron products (bars, plates, rails) until after 1750, so its early use was limited to a specialized casting process patented by Darby. Between 1750 and 1790, coke iron replaced charcoal iron in making rolled products. Coke iron was still too expensive to oust charcoal smelting on the continent, however, for countries like

France were endowed with extensive forests providing cheap charcoal and suffered from scarce and expensive coal. It took a further 50 years of improvement in blast furnace design to raise the productivity of coke furnaces sufficiently for them to out-compete charcoal in continental Europe. That transition occurred rapidly in the 1860s as French and German firms built blast furnaces of the most advanced design. They leapt, in other words, to the cutting edge of iron technology since that was the only form of the technology that was competitive there.

Likewise, the continent did not lag behind Britain in the new industries of the mid-19th century. Western Europe built railways, and Europe's locomotives were as advanced as Britain's. The same was true of steel. Before 1850, steel was an expensive – and minor – product of the iron industry, which mainly produced plates and rails from wrought iron refined from pig iron in the puddling furnace. The technical problem in steel production was to melt pure pig iron, so that the addition of other elements including carbon could be precisely controlled. A temperature in excess of 1500° C was required. The first solution was the converter, invented independently around 1850 by Henry Bessemer and William Kelly. An alternative solution was pioneered by Sir Carl Wilhelm Siemens, who built a regenerative furnace in the 1850s that could reach very high temperatures. In 1865, Pierre-Émile Martin used the Siemens furnace to melt pig iron to make steel. The so-called open hearth furnace proved superior to the Bessemer converter in the production of plates, sheets, and structural shapes, and became the dominant technology until it was superseded by the basic oxygen process in the 1960s. The important point is that the four inventors of mass-produced steel were an Englishman, an American, a German living in England, and a Frenchman. There was no international lag there.

While Western Europe had overcome its most glaring technological deficiencies by 1870, production levels on the continent were still far behind those of Britain. This changed by the First World War, however, as both Western Europe and the USA overtook Britain in manufacturing. In 1880, Britain produced 23% of the world's manufactures, while France, Germany, and Belgium together produced only 18%. By 1913, the three continental countries had out-paced Britain as their share rose to 23% and Britain's share dropped to 14%. At the same time, the North American share grew from 15% to 33% of world manufacturing. Britain did best in the cotton textile industry, processing 869,000 tons of raw cotton per year in 1905–13, against the USA which reached 1,110,000 tons, Germany 435,000, and France 231,000. British performance was far weaker in heavy industry. In 1850–4, Britain smelted 3 million tons of pig iron versus 245,000 in Germany and about 500,000 in the USA. By 1910–13, Britain was producing 10 million tons, while Germany smelted 15 million, and the USA 24 million.

The changes in manufacturing production had important political implications. In the middle of the 19th century, Britain was the 'workshop of the world', producing most of the world's exported manufactures. The USA and Germany, in particular, increased their production of manufactures by increasing their exports, and the changes in trade performance were widely discussed. Britain continued to hold its own in selling to its empire, and the value of empire demonstrated in that way led to a scramble for colonies among the industrial economies. Germany's overtaking of Britain in steel production had implications for armaments manufacture. The Anglo-German trade rivalry stoked international tensions in the approach to the First World War.

Not only did continental Europe and North America overtake Britain in industrial output between 1870 and 1913, but they manifestly joined it in technological competence. The USA, indeed, surpassed Britain, becoming the world's technological leader. In most industries, however, important discoveries were made in all of the leading industrial economies. From the global perspective, what is striking is the difference between the rich countries, who, as a group, pushed technology forward, and the rest of the world, which seemingly made no innovations at all.

An important feature of the late 19th century was the development of entirely new industries – automobiles, petroleum, electricity, chemicals. All of the rich countries were involved in creating these industries. The first vehicle powered by a gasoline engine was built by Siegfried Marcus, an Austrian, in 1870. He also invented a magneto ignition system and rotating brush carburettor that have become standards. Karl Benz built the first practical automobile in 1885, closely followed by Gottlieb Daimler and Wilhelm Maybach. They were Germans. William Lanchester built the first British auto in 1895 and invented the disc brake and electric starter. The first company organized expressly to manufacture autos was Panhard et Levassor in France in 1889. They also invented the four-cylinder engine. Renault introduced drum brakes in 1902. In 1903, Jacobus Spijker of the Netherlands built the first four-wheel-drive racing vehicle. Automobiles required a range of innovations covering engines, starting systems, brakes, transmissions, suspensions, electrics, and so forth. The modern auto is the result of inventions made by people in all of the leading industrial countries. By 1900, all of the industrial countries had firms manufacturing autos. Innovation was a collective activity among them.

Another feature of the new industries was that many were related to developments in the natural sciences. Countries with strong university programmes in these areas reaped economic benefits. Germany is the pre-eminent example before the 1930s. Its physicists and chemists won many Nobel Prizes. Key technical personnel in industry were trained in universities, and their academic staff made important discoveries that improved industrial processes and led to new products. Fritz Haber's discovery of the process to convert atmospheric nitrogen to ammonia, made when he was at the University of Karlsruhe and for which he received a Nobel Prize, is one of the most famous, but far from unique.

Hitler, the Second World War, and post-war division derailed German science. The lead in university research passed to the USA, which had been developing a very large higher education sector. University research in the USA floated on a sea of government money. This was directed towards the military during the Cold War, but many of the projects brought benefits to the economy as a whole. Funding was also directed towards medicine, space exploration, and even the humanities and social sciences. This funding underpinned America's global leadership.

The macro-economic character of technological progress

Most R&D has been carried out in today's rich countries. They have developed technologies that they anticipated would be profitable. Therefore, the new products and processes that they pioneered were addressed to their needs and suited to their circumstances; in particular, the high wages of rich countries induced them to invent products that economized on labour by increasing the use of capital. This led to an ascending spiral of progress: high wages induced more capital-intensive production that, in turn, led to higher wages. This spiral underlies the rising incomes of rich countries.

A consequence of Western Europe and the USA doing all of the world's R&D is that there is a world 'production function' that defines the technological options of all countries. A 'production function' is the mathematical relationship that indicates how much GDP a country can produce with its labour and capital. Figure 8 shows the world production function by plotting GDP per worker against capital per worker for 57 countries in 1965 and 1990. The points bracket the function. It has the feature that more capital per worker translates into more output per worker. Moreover, the

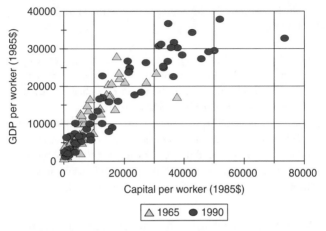

8. World production function

relationship flattens out at high levels of capital per worker because of the law of diminishing returns: more and more capital yields less and less additional output. Finally, different icons are used for the 1965 and the 1990 data. A country with $10,000 of capital per worker produced no more output in 1990 than it did in 1965. It experienced no technical progress, in other words. The change in the world's technology consisted in getting more output per worker by pushing capital per worker to levels higher than those reached before. The beneficiaries of these improvements were the rich countries operating with highly capital-intensive technologies in 1965. These were also the countries that invented the new technologies of 1990. These improvements did not automatically trickle down to poorer countries.

For some of these countries, we can measure output per worker and capital per worker back to the Industrial Revolution. With these data, we can compare what has happened *over time* to what happens *across space*. For instance, the line in Figure 9 labelled 'USA' connects the points representing capital per worker and output per worker for the USA from 1820 to 1990. The trajectory of the USA's development follows the same pattern as rich and poor countries in 1965 and 1990. It is the same story for all other rich countries: growth over time looks like differences across space today. Figure 10 shows this for Italy, and Figure 11 for Germany. There are some idiosyncrasies in these histories – the USA, as befits the world's technological leader, has usually got a bit more output from its capital and labour than other countries, while Germany, perhaps because of the importance of investment banks, has accumulated more capital per worker – but the fundamental dynamics are the same. The correspondence between growth over time and differences across space is a direct consequence of the fact that the technological possibilities in the world today were created by the rich countries as they developed.

The reason that poor countries are poor is because they use technology that was developed by rich countries in the past. The most successful industry of many developing countries is the manufacture of clothing. The key technology is the sewing machine. The treadle sewing machine was first produced commercially in the 1850s, and the electric sewing machine was

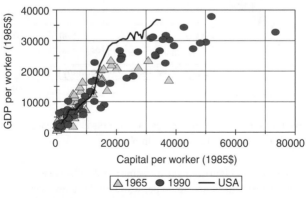

9. US growth trajectory

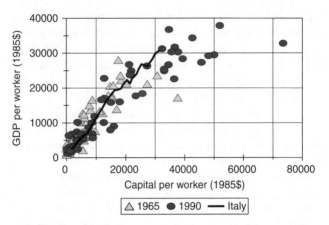

10. Italian growth trajectory

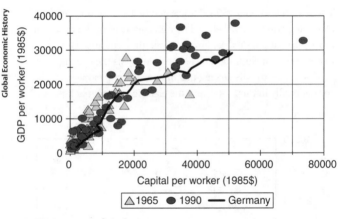

11. German growth trajectory

introduced in 1889. Export success in most developing countries today is based on 19th-century technology.

The statistics in Figure 8 make the same point. Why is Peru relatively poor? In 1990, capital per worker in Peru was $8,796 and output per worker was $6,847. These figures are almost identical to Germany's in 1913: $8,769 and $6,425, respectively. Less capital today throws you further back in time. In 1990, for instance, Zimbabwe had $3,823 of capital per worker, and each worker produced $2,537 per year. Not bad for 1820. Malawi had $428 of capital, and GDP per worker was $1,217 – about the same as India early in the 19th century, and considerably below the levels realized in the UK, USA, and Western Europe at the same time. Even in 1990, capital per worker in India had increased only to $1,946 and output per worker had reached $3,235 – putting India on a par with Britain in 1820.

The obvious question is why Peru, Zimbabwe, Malawi, and India do not adopt the technology of the Western countries and become rich themselves. The answer is that it would not pay. Western technology in the 21st century uses vast amounts of capital per worker. It only pays to substitute that much capital for labour when wages are high relative to capital costs. This is shown in all Figures by the flattening out of the relationship between output per worker and capital per worker. When capital per worker is high, it takes a lot more capital per worker to increase output per worker by $1,000 than is required when capital per worker is low. Labour has to be very expensive to make it worthwhile to build all that extra capital. The Western countries have experienced a development trajectory in which higher wages led to the invention of labour-saving technology, whose use drove up labour productivity and wages with it. The cycle repeats. Today's poor countries missed the elevator. They have low wages and high capital costs, so they make do with archaic technology and low incomes.

Industrial history provides examples of these principles. In the last chapter, we discussed the invention of the power loom and the way it was brought into use in the USA – a very high-wage country – and then in Britain, once it was perfected. The power loom was never cost-effective in low-wage countries, where people continued to weave with hand looms. Their situation became even more difficult later in the 19th century when the USA became the economic leader with the highest wage economy. American technology reflected that circumstance. In the 1890s, an English immigrant named James Henry Northrop made a series of inventions that resulted in a fully automatic loom. It greatly increased labour productivity but required substantial investment. These looms were profitable to install in America where wages were very high, but they were too expensive to use in Britain – even though Britain was a high-wage economy by world standards. The Northrop loom was even less appropriate in poor countries. The process of technical change, in which inventors in the leading economies sought to save high-wage labour, resulted in machinery that further increased the competitive advantage of rich countries without conferring any advantage on the poor countries of the world.

Chapter 5
The great empires

To the east of Europe were empires. The Ottoman Turks conquered Constantinople in 1453, and their rule extended from the Balkans, to the Middle East and North Africa. The writ of the Russian Tsar ran from Poland to Vladivostok. The Persian Empire, under different dynasties, lasted for thousands of years. Much of India was governed by the Mughal emperors in the 17th and 18th centuries. Japan had an emperor from the 3rd century CE onwards, and parts of South Asia such as Cambodia and Thailand had advanced states from an early date. China was the greatest empire of all and had existed for thousands of years.

Europeans have been aware of the riches of Asia for millennia, and that was one reason they tried to sail there. Marco Polo's account of his 13th-century journey to China was popular, and Columbus annotated his personal copy. Jean-Baptiste Du Halde's *Description de la Chine* (1736), based on Jesuit missionary accounts, painted a glowing picture of Chinese civilization. It was widely read and debated.

Not everyone accepted that the East was prosperous, however. Leading the doubters were the classical economists Adam Smith, Robert Malthus, and Karl Marx. They agreed that Europe was richer and had better prospects for growth. Each explained China's hypothesized backwardness with his own pet theory – for

Smith, the problem was the state prohibition on foreign trade and a suspected insecurity of private property; for Malthus, it was universal marriage that resulted in high fertility and consequently low incomes; for Marx, it was a pre-capitalist social structure that failed to sustain individual initiative.

These views became widely accepted, but have been challenged in recent years by the California School of economic history – so called because its proponents are professors at California universities. According to the California School, China's legal system was comparable to Europe's and property was secure, the Chinese family system kept the fertility rate low so that the population grew no more rapidly in China than in Europe, markets for commodities and for land, labour, and capital were as evolved as those in Europe. As a result, productivity and living standards were similar at both ends of Eurasia. The reason that the Industrial Revolution happened in Europe does not, therefore, lie in institutional or cultural differences but rather in the continent's accessible coal reserves and gains from globalization.

This re-interpretation has been widely debated for both China and for other empires. Most doubtful is the suggestion that the advanced parts of China like the Yangzi Delta had incomes as high as those of England and the Netherlands (Figure 3). On the other hand, the positive assessment of Chinese markets and institutions gains credence since reassessments of other empires (such as that of Rome) have come to similar conclusions, and the California School is right that the Industrial Revolution happened in Britain because of coal and commerce. What is notable about Asian history is the absence of such triggers.

Globalization and de-industrialization

Few of the great empires had a good 19th century. India formally became a British colony after the Mutiny of 1857. The Chinese, Ottoman, and Russian emperors were overthrown by the 1920s.

The great empires started the 19th century with the largest manufacturing industries in the world and ended the century with these industries destroyed and without modern factory industries to replace them. The only – and partial – exceptions were Russia and Japan.

Three factors drove economic success and failure between Waterloo and the Second World War – technology, globalization, and state policy.

The Industrial Revolution in the West drove Asian manufacturers out of business for two reasons. First, manufacturing became more productive in Europe, cutting costs there. Industrial technology, however, was not cost-effective in other parts of the world where wages were lower. There was no point, for instance, in the Indians trying to compete against English textiles by using spinning machines since they increased the capital costs of spinning *in India* more than they lowered the labour costs. Asian producers either had to hope that the British would improve spinning machines sufficiently to make them cost-effective in Asia (which eventually did happen) or redesign the machines to adapt them to their own circumstances (which is what Japan did).

Second, steamships and railways made international competition more intense. As transportation costs fell, the world economy became more and more tightly integrated, and Western firms using power-driven machinery were able to out-compete producers using handicraft methods from Casablanca to Canton – despite the great difference in wages. As manufacturing disappeared in Asia and the Middle East, their labour forces were redeployed into agriculture, and these continents became exporters of wheat, cotton, rice, and other primary products. They became, in other words, modern underdeveloped countries.

These developments were not due to a conspiracy among the rich nor simply to colonialism (although it played a role). They were the result of one of the fundamental principles of economics – comparative advantage. According to this theory, countries that trade with each other specialize in the production of commodities that they can produce relatively efficiently. They export those goods and import the ones that they produce relatively inefficiently. Suppose India, for instance, were cut off from the rest of the world. The only way to increase its consumption of cotton cloth would be by reducing employment in farming and shifting the workers to spinning and weaving. The efficiency of labour in these activities would determine how much wheat had to be given up to get another metre of cloth. If it became possible to trade internationally, and if the price of cloth relative to wheat in the world market was less than the ratio implied by domestic production techniques, then Indians would have found it advantageous to export wheat and import cloth rather than producing the cloth themselves. They would, in other words, have become farmers rather than manufacturers. This reconfiguration brought short-run prosperity at the cost of long-run development.

Before Vasco da Gama reached Calicut, market connections between Europe and Asia were tenuous. Each continent was effectively 'cut off from the rest of the world'. This isolation evaporated with the development of the square-rigged sailing ship, global navigation, the steamship, the Suez Canal, the railway, the telegraph, the Panama Canal, the automobile, the aeroplane, the container ship, the telephone, the motorway, the Internet. All of these have reduced the costs of international transactions, integrated markets, and brought countries into more intense competition with each other. The principle of comparative advantage has come more powerfully into play, and the differences in the relative efficiency of production have become of greater and greater moment in determining the wealth of nations. The result has been the 'underdevelopment' of the Third World.

Government policy was the third factor affecting economic performance after Waterloo. The USA and Western Europe met the challenge of cheap British imports with the standard development strategy of internal improvements, external tariffs, investment banks, and universal education. Colonies were not in a position to entertain such a strategy since their economic policies were subordinated to the interests of the colonial power. Independent states had the option of pursuing national development, although not all of them made the effort or succeeded in it.

Cotton textiles

We can see these themes in action in the history of cotton textile production in India and Britain. The productivity of cotton production in Britain rose during the Industrial Revolution as machinery was perfected. An increase in British manufacturing productivity that was not matched by an equal increase in India was bound to increase the competitiveness of English cotton manufacturers while reducing the competitiveness of Indian manufacturers, according to the principle of comparative advantage. Conversely, India's comparative advantage in the production of agricultural goods should have increased, while England's declined. Comparative advantage implies that the unbalanced productivity growth of the Industrial Revolution should have furthered industrial development in England, while de-industrializing India. And that is what happened.

The shift of comparative advantage occurred in an age of falling transport costs, which intensified the ramifications. Transport costs declined as the efficiency of ships improved and because of increased competition on the sea routes from Europe to India. In the 18th century, this trade was dominated by the English and Dutch East Indies companies. While their appearance in the early 17th century had shattered Portuguese control of the pepper trade and led to a fall in its price in Europe, the British Navigation Acts kept the Dutch out of the English market and checked further competition. The Fourth Anglo-Dutch War (1780–4) was the final blow: the Dutch company was so weakened that its charter was allowed to expire in 1800. Finally, the English company lost its trading monopoly in 1813. The resulting increase in competition led to falling transport costs between India and Europe.

The effect of unbalanced productivity growth and declining shipping costs shows up in the histories of cotton prices in England and India. In 1812, a group of English cotton manufacturers met to oppose the extension of the East India Company's trade monopoly. They prepared a memorandum that showed 40-count yarn cost 43 pence per pound to spin in India but only 30 pence in England. The conclusion was that India was a great potential market for British products if only competition were allowed. They were right. It is remarkable, however, that they could not have made this argument even ten years earlier, since at that time British 40-count yarn cost 60 pence per pound. The technology of 1802 was not sufficiently productive to undercut India. The machines of 1812 could do that. The machines continued to be improved, and by 1826, the price of 40-count yarn had dropped to 16 pence. At that price, not even the poorest woman in India found it worthwhile to spin, and Indian production of cotton yarn evaporated until mechanized factories were set up in the 1870s.

The story was repeated with weaving, but the results were not quite as catastrophic for India. Technological progress drove down the price of English calico, as discussed in Chapter 4. From the mid-1780s, English cloth was always cheaper in England than Indian cloth. Their prices could not drift too far apart, however, since buyers regarded them as good substitutes for each other. Hence, the drop in the English price after 1790 dragged the Indian price down with it (Figure 12).

There is a gap in our Indian price series between 1805 and 1818, but in that interval, two momentous changes occurred. First, the difference between prices in India and England became very

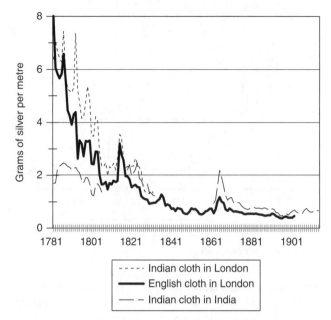

12. Real price of cotton

small. The markets were integrated, so that developments in one affected the other. Second, English prices fell below Indian prices. Cloth exports from India to England dried up since there was no longer money to be made in that direction. Instead, England exported to India.

The impact on India was large. The country shifted from being a major exporter to a major importer. The spinning industry was wholly destroyed, and India imported all its cotton yarn. Weaving output also declined, although hand-loom weaving survived on a smaller and less remunerative scale. In Bihar, the share of the work force in manufacturing dropped from 22% around 1810 to 9% in 1901. This was de-industrialization big time!

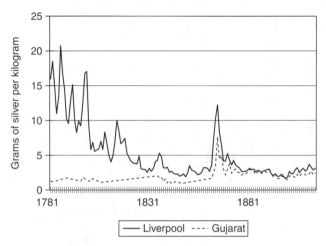

13. **Real price of raw cotton**

Every country has a comparative advantage in something. As India lost its advantage in manufacturing, it gained an advantage in agriculture – raw cotton, in particular. Figure 13 shows the real price of raw cotton in Gujarat and in Liverpool from 1781 to 1913. In the 18th century, cotton was much cheaper in India. Cotton prices fell in Britain, as cotton cultivation in the southern USA expanded. By the 1830s, the English and Indian markets were integrated. While integration in the yarn and cloth markets resulted in declining prices that forced Indian manufacturers out of business, the reverse was true in agriculture. The price of raw cotton rose gradually, leading to an expansion of cultivation and exports of raw cotton to supply the British textile industry.

In a sharp exchange before the British Parliament's Select Committee on East India Produce in 1840, Mr John Brocklehurst, MP for Macclesfield, put it to the witness Robert Montgomery Martin that 'the destruction of weaving in India had already taken place', so that 'India is an agricultural rather than a manufacturing country, and that the parties formerly employed in manufactures are now absorbed in agriculture'. Martin, who was a critic of the British Empire, replied:

> I do not agree that India is an agricultural country; India is as much a manufacturing country as an agricultural, and he who would seek to reduce her to the position of an agricultural country seeks to lower her in the scale of civilization … her manufactures of various descriptions have existed for ages, and have never been able to be competed with by any nation wherever fair play has been given to them.

However laudable were Martin's sentiments, the market forces were on Brocklehurst's side, and British industry out-competed Indian manufacturing.

The story of Indian textiles was the story of much of the Third World in the 19th century. Biased technical change in combination with globalization promoted the industrialization of Western countries while simultaneously de-industrializing the ancient manufacturing economies of Asia. Even when nations were independent – the Ottoman Empire is an example – technical change and falling transport costs turned them into modern underdeveloped countries. In the mid-20th century, the problem of Asian economic development was conceived as a problem of modernizing 'traditional societies'. In fact, their circumstances were anything but traditional. Underdevelopment was the product of 19th-century globalization and Western industrial development.

Modern industry in India

Was India destined to remain a less developed country that exported primary products and imported manufactures? Or would the elimination of handicraft production be followed by industrial development as modern factories were built to take advantage of India's low-wage labour force? Indian history is an especially important experiment in answering these questions, for India had the benefit of British rule, British law, and British free trade. Did they help it or hurt it?

India did experience some industrial development. The notable successes were the jute and cotton industries. Both took advantage of cheap Indian labour. British investors financed the growth of jute mills in Bengal, and by the First World War, the industry was the largest in the world, and its exports had driven British competitors out of most markets. The cotton industry flourished in Bombay, and by 1913, it was processing 360,000 tons of raw cotton per year – more than France but less than Germany. These successes had only a negligible impact on the national economy, however. Employment in cotton and jute mills amounted to half a million people in 1911, or well under 1% of the labour force. The economy remained overwhelmingly agricultural.

Industrial development required moving the economy away from the pattern dictated by comparative advantage. The nationalist view is that India needed the standard development policies that helped Western Europe and the USA catch up to Britain – that is, tariffs, investment banks, internal improvements, and universal schools.

What is most striking about colonial rule is how little this programme was pursued. In the 19th century, only 1% of the Indian population was in school, and the literacy rate of the adult population was 6%. Tariffs were low and only for revenue purposes. There was no banking policy to finance industry.

The initiatives undertaken by the Indian government highlight the limitations of its policy. Regions like the Punjab were irrigated to increase agricultural exports. Railways were promoted after the Mutiny in 1857 to move troops around the country and to connect interior agricultural districts to the coast to facilitate exporting primary products. In the event, 61,000 kilometres of track were laid before the First World War, giving India one of the largest rail networks in the world. The railways did create a national market, since goods could be shipped across India at low cost.

Building India's railways must, however, be regarded as a missed opportunity. Railways were huge projects that required modern inputs like steel rails and locomotives. Most countries ensured that railroad building would enlarge or even create these industries by using tariffs and procurement requirements to channel the orders to local firms. Instead, the colonial government made sure that the orders went to British firms. Exports of British engineering goods to India surged. There was, however, no spin-off to India, and the founding of the country's iron and engineering industries waited until the 20th century.

Even today, agricultural employment predominates in India, Pakistan, and Bangladesh, and this is the case in other poor countries. Some countries that were poor in the 19th century, however, did much better in the 20th by following the standard strategy and also by going beyond it to effect a Big Push, as we shall see.

Chapter 6
The Americas

The incorporation of the Americas into the global economy has had enormous ramifications for the Old World and the New. The native American population collapsed, and indigenous civilizations were replaced by European. Northern Europe was propelled towards industrialization, and the Americas themselves exemplify the worldwide split between a rich North and a poor South.

The different development trajectories of North and South America run back to the colonial period and are rooted in geography and demography. South America contained most of the indigenous population and had the greatest wealth. It was also further from Europe. These differences cumulated into the difference in income that we see today.

Geography mattered because it affected the ability to trade with Europe. Trade could be good or bad for economic growth. On the one hand, cheap British manufactures inhibited industrialization; on the other, exporting local agricultural products powerfully promoted settlement and farming generally, and these could be springboards to later industrialization. North America was favoured in this regard. First, it was closer to Europe, which was the main market for colonial exports. With shipping costs high, North Americans could profitably produce and export a wider range of products than South Americans. This advantage was reinforced by the interior geography of the continents. The eastern seaboard of North America was broad enough and fertile enough to support a significant economy, and the interior of the continent could be reached by the St Lawrence, Mohawk-Hudson, and Mississippi Rivers. In contrast, most economic activity in Latin America was in the interior of Mexico and the Andes. Rivers did not connect these regions to the coast, so the cost of exporting was high.

Demography was also important. The temperate climate of most of the USA, Canada, and much of South America presented little disease threat to Europeans, so they flourished in those regions. In contrast, tropical diseases led to high European mortality in the Caribbean and Amazon and depressed the growth of the European population.

The native population was distributed unevenly across the Americas. Most natives lived in Mexico (21 million) or the Andes (12 million); only about 5 million lived in the USA, with only 250,000 in the original 13 colonies. The difference in population reflected geography. Mexico and Peru were the habitats of the natural progenitors of the main native foods – maize, beans, squash, potatoes, and quinoa. These plants were domesticated where they grew in the wild and, consequently, were well adapted to those environments. In addition, farmers there cultivated them earlier than anywhere else. Maize and beans, for instance, were domesticated 4,700 years ago, and so there were 4,200 years for the Mexican population to grow in response before Cortés arrived in 1519. Of course, maize, beans, and squash diffused widely, but their genetics and cultivation had to be adapted to different environments, which slowed their spread. The growing season of maize, for instance, had to be cut from the 120–150 days characteristic of the tropics to about 100 days or less for it to succeed in colder climates, and that task was not accomplished until about 1000 CE. Nowhere in the eastern half of the USA or

Canada was maize widely cultivated before that date, so the population of eastern North America had little time to grow before the Europeans turned up.

The arrival of Europeans was a catastrophe for the natives. A mid-range estimate of their population in 1500 is 57 million; by 1750, it had dropped to perhaps 5 million. Much of the decline was due to the introduction of diseases such as smallpox, measles, influenza, and typhus for which the natives had no immunity. The rest was down to war, enslavement, and ill treatment by the settlers.

The implications of this drop, which was common to all natives, differed in North and South America because the pre-contact populations differed in size. In Mexico, the native population declined by over 90%, reaching a low point of 750,000 in the 1620s. This was still three times the population on the east coast of the USA before European arrival. In the Andes, the native population dropped below 600,000 after an epidemic in 1718–20. The native population in Mexico rebounded after the mid-17th century, reaching 3.5 million in 1800, and the native population of the Andes reached 2 million. Despite the Spanish immigration in the previous three centuries, the natives comprised three-fifths of the population of these regions, and people of mixed race amounted to another fifth. The final fifth were the relatively well-off whites, who ruled these colonies. This racial and economic structure had negative implications for long-run growth.

The situation was very different in North America because there were few natives to begin with. The quarter-million living on the east coast in 1500 were reduced to only 14,697 in 1890, when they were fully enumerated in the US census for the first time. Most of the fall occurred in the 17th century and, indeed, often before European settlement. The Pilgrims' landing in Massachusetts in 1620 was preceded by epidemics in 1617–19. The Pilgrims saw this as God's blessing: 'Thus farre hath the good hand of God favored our beginnings…In sweeping away great multitudes of the natives…a little more before we went thither, that he might make room for us there.' Fifty years of warfare eliminated the rest. High mortality among the natives and low mortality among the settlers meant that the American colonies became a transplantation of England very rapidly. The obvious exceptions to this generalization were the southern US colonies, where the Europeans imported African slaves to do the hard work. But the survival of natives did not affect development in North America as it did south of the Rio Grande.

Colonial economy of North America

Settlement is the theme of the colonial history of the USA. Some settlers, particularly in New England, were motivated by the desire to create their own religious autocracy rather than submit to the hegemony of another creed. Most settlers, however, were motivated by economic gain, and even the Puritans expected to earn the same standard of living in Massachusetts that they could have realized in England.

Settlement and exporting were closely connected in British North America. The Canadian economist Harold Innis highlighted the relationship with his 'staples thesis', which contended that the growth of a region like Canada was determined by the growth of its exports – cod fish, furs, timber – to Europe. Sales of these products provided the money to buy manufactured goods like cloth, tools, crockery, books, and so on. These were imported from Britain, rather than produced in the colony, since British industries were large and realized economies of scale that meant they could produce more efficiently than small, colonial firms. 'The Farmers deem it better for their profit to put away [i.e. exchange] their cattle and corn for cloathing, then to set upon making of cloth.' Britain's Navigation Acts prevented the Dutch and the French from supplying the colonies' needs.

Staple colonies had three characteristics. First, the price of the staple in the colony was less than its price in Europe by an amount that equalled the transportation cost. Prices in the two markets moved up and down together since they were linked by trade. Second, exports amounted to a large share of colonial income, with the remainder being support services. Third, the returns to settlers and their capital exceeded returns in Europe by a margin covering the costs and risks of moving to the colony.

Pennsylvania illustrates these principles. The colony was founded in 1681 and was suited to the cultivation of wheat, which became its staple. Pennsylvania exports competed with Irish and English produce in the West Indies, Iberia, and the British Isles. As a result, prices in Philadelphia and London moved up and down together. The synchronization is apparent in Figure 14. The Seven Years War (1756–63) and the American Revolution (1776–83)

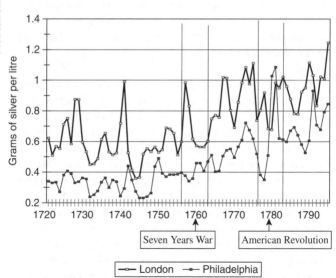

14. **Price of wheat**

were the exceptions that prove the rule, for trade was disrupted in these periods, and the correlation of prices broke down. In addition to wheat and flour, the colony exported timber products, ships, iron, and potash, and earned foreign exchange from its merchant marine. Exports were important to the colony's economy and amounted to about 30% of total output in 1770. The foreign exchange earned on these sales paid for English consumer goods.

As the economy grew, it attracted more labour from Europe. In the 18th century, Philadelphia real wages followed the English trend but at a higher level to compensate the colonists for the cost of relocating to a remote wilderness (Figure 15). England and its North American colonies were prosperous places, with wages four to five times subsistence – in contrast to cities like Florence where wages dropped to bare-bones subsistence at the end of the 18th century.

The economy of New England performed less satisfactorily, as Figure 15 suggests. In the early 18th century, wages in

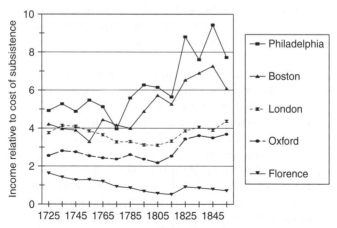

15. Wages of an unskilled labourer, Europe and USA

Massachusetts were on a par with London but lower than in Pennsylvania. While Massachusetts holds an iconic place in popular views of American history, its economy was always precarious because it lacked an agricultural staple. An export trade was developed in fish, livestock, whale oil, and wood products including ships. New Englanders also created a large shipping industry that generated substantial foreign earnings and annoyed the English mercantilists since it competed with the Mother Country. These activities did not expand rapidly, so the demand for labour in New England increased less rapidly than the natural increase of the population. As a result, wages sagged, and there was continual out-migration.

While the staples thesis was developed to explain Canada, the best examples are the sugar colonies of the Caribbean. Europeans first encountered sugar on Crusade in Palestine. After their expulsion, production was shifted to Cyprus, and eventually, it was cultivated on islands in the Atlantic. The Portuguese occupation of São Tomé in 1485 was a turning point, for there they pioneered cultivation on large plantations staffed by African slaves. This system was later introduced to Brazil and the Caribbean where it proved immensely profitable. In the 17th and 18th centuries, Barbados, Jamaica, Cuba, and Saint Domingue (now Haiti) were amongst the wealthiest places in the world.

A Caribbean colony grew sugar and other crops like coffee and exported the produce to Europe. The necessary capital and labour were supplied by European investors and African slaves, who proved to be a cheaper source of labour than European immigrants. Mortality on sugar plantations was very high, and new slaves were so cheap that the slaves were replenished by purchase rather than natural increase. Four million slaves were taken to the British West Indies, for instance, but only 400,000 were present at emancipation in 1832. The volume of exports determined the size of the colonial economy. In Jamaica in 1832, for instance, exports of sugar, coffee, and other tropical produce added up to 41% of the island's income. The rest was support activities for the plantations (the production of food for the slaves, other supplies, shipping, and transport services, the forces of law and order, and housing for the ancillary workers) or the consumption expenditures of the planters on domestic servants and country houses. The planters' expenditures in the colony were only a small part of their incomes, most of which was repatriated to Britain rather than being invested in Jamaica.

Many features of the Caribbean were replicated in the southern colonies of the future USA. The South had the valuable staples – rice and indigo in South Carolina, and tobacco in Virginia and Maryland. These crops were produced on plantations initially staffed by English indentured servants and eventually by African slaves. The South was richer than the northern colonies and attracted more settlers and was the destination of most slaves.

South Carolina, for instance, was first settled in 1670. However, the settlers lacked 'any Commodityes fit for the market of Europe but a few Skins they purchased from the native Indians and a little Cedar with which they helpe to fill the ship that brings the skins for London'. In the next decades, they searched for a staple and eventually stumbled on rice. Exports rose from 69 pounds per head in 1700 to 900 pounds in 1740. Imports of slaves jumped from 275 per year to 2,000 over the same decades. Experimentation with cultivation techniques increased land and labour productivity by half. The social structure of coastal areas where the rice was grown became increasingly like the Caribbean sugar islands. Exports added up to more than 30% of total coastal income. The economy revolved around rice as Jamaica's revolved around sugar. The population became overwhelmingly black.

The white population, which was half the total in the lower South, retreated towards the interior, where family farms predominated. While they grew their own food, they were far from self-sufficient since they supplied the rice plantations with food and used the proceeds to purchase English cloth and other consumer goods. Virginia and Maryland worked similarly with tobacco as the export staple.

The British colonies differed greatly in terms of economic and social inequality. New England and the Middle Atlantic colonies were the most egalitarian. Some slaves were present, but slavery was unimportant in agriculture – not because of moral scruples or technical difficulties but because slaves would not have generated enough income to cover their cost. The abundance of land kept down its price and meant that most income accrued as wages, which were necessarily widely distributed. At the other extreme were the Caribbean colonies, where most of the population were slaves and inequality was extreme. The colonies of the Southern USA were intermediate cases that combined the inequality of the plantation with the egalitarianism of small-scale farmers on the frontier.

The economies of the North American colonies did, however, share one advantage that bode well for their future – namely, the literacy of white settlers was at least as high as in England, which was near the top of the world league table (Table 4). By the Revolution, 70% of free men in Virginia and Pennsylvania could sign their names, compared to 65% in England at the same time. In New England, the rate was close to 90%, which was achieved through state schools and mandatory attendance.

Why was literacy high in the colonies? For the same reason it was high in England: economic advantage. The dependence of the colonists' standard of living on trade and foreign markets meant that reading, writing, and calculation brought rewards. The legal system also made literacy valuable since contracts and land titles were written documents. The Puritans' desire to read the Bible may have played a role in pushing Massachusetts literacy above that in England or Pennsylvania, but the dependence of their economy on trade and shipping gave them a powerful economic motive for schooling.

Colonial economy of Latin America

Different regions of Latin America followed different development trajectories from the future USA, and none of them did as well. We need to distinguish (1) the Caribbean and Brazil, (2) the southern cone (Argentina, Chile, Uruguay), and (3) Mexico and the Andes.

We have already discussed the Caribbean economies, and similar developments occurred in Brazil, only on an expanded scale reflecting its greater size. It was close enough to Europe to export sugar, which the Portuguese introduced from Saõ Tomé in the early 16th century. Initially, the plantations were operated with native American slaves, but Africans were soon substituted, and the first staple boom was underway. Between 1580 and 1660, Portugal and Spain were united. The Dutch war against Spain was extended to Portugal, and from 1630 to 1654, the Dutch occupied Pernambuco, the sugar-growing province of Brazil. When they left, they took the knowledge of sugar production with them, and its cultivation was introduced into the Caribbean. Caribbean producers were closer to Europe and could undercut their rivals in Brazil: the price of sugar in Amsterdam dropped from three-quarters of a guilder per pound in 1589 to one-quarter of a guilder in 1688. Brazilian plantations could not compete at that price, and the Brazilian sugar boom was over. The country's economic history for the next three centuries was one staple boom after the other: gold (early 18th century), coffee (1840–1930), rubber (1879–1912). In each case, a product was shipped to Europe, and slaves or settlers were brought in to cultivate it. Like sugar in the Caribbean – but unlike the USA – Brazil's staple booms never turned into modern economic growth: why not?

The southern cone of Latin America was like North America in that it had a small native population that was killed off by disease, warfare, and European mistreatment. The Pampas could produce beef and wheat at least as well as Pennsylvania, but Argentina was too far from Europe for that to be feasible in the colonial period. All that Argentina could muster was a small export trade in hides. Chile was even more remote. The economic history of these countries began in earnest only in the middle of the 19th century, when ships were sufficiently improved for their exports to compete in Europe.

The most important Spanish colonies were Mexico and the Andes. Their histories were determined by conquest. While the North American settlers encountered natives practising slash-and-burn cultivation in a sparsely settled landscape, the Spanish found dense populations, great cities, productive agriculture, political and religious organization as hierarchical as their own, and hoards of gold and silver. The *conquistadores* overthrew the Aztec and Inca rulers and put themselves in their place. The gold and silver were looted. The native religions were suppressed, their texts burnt, and Catholicism established in their stead. The natives were reduced to a subservient race whose purpose was to support the conquerors. Hundreds of thousands of Spaniards went to America to seek their fortunes.

The Aztecs and Incas had exploited their subjects with demands of tribute and labour, and the Spanish did the same. Native wages were extraordinarily low: in the 1530s, a fully employed Mexican native would have earned only one-quarter of the cost of a subsistence basket of goods (Figure 16). This was not enough for a family to survive. The abuses were so severe that in 1542 the Spanish Crown prohibited aboriginal slavery and limited the power of the *conquistadores*.

Meanwhile, the native population collapsed, but enough survived to make their continued exploitation worthwhile. Forced labour was one strategy. In the 1570s, the *mita*, which had been an Inca system of labour conscription, was revived to provide workers for the silver mines at Potosi. Mexico followed Aztec precedents with its own form of forced labour, the *repartimento*. The Crown also

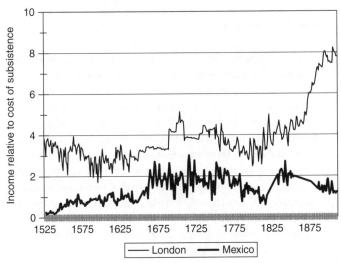

16. **Wages of an unskilled labourer, Mexico and London**

granted unoccupied land to Spaniards as estates called haciendas. By the early 17th century, more than half of the agricultural land in the valley of Mexico had been acquired by rich Spaniards in this way. The rest of the land was owned communally by native bands, who practised shifting cultivation. A large native population occupying land under communal tenure had no parallel in the North American colonies.

Another important difference from North America was geography, which prevented Peru and Mexico from exporting agricultural staples. It is not surprising that Peru was too far from Europe for this to happen. Indeed, the markets on the west coast of America were better integrated with Asia than with Europe. The Spanish ran galleons between Acapulco and Manila, swapping silver coins for Chinese silk and tea. In the late 18th century, 'numerous French, English, and American vessels' bought seal skins from the natives of present-day British Columbia and sold them in China.

'The price of the skins, as they rose on the coast of America, fell enormously in China.'

Mexico is more puzzling. Vera Cruz, its port on the Caribbean, was no further from Europe than New Orleans. The problem for Mexico, however, was the high cost of moving goods between the sea and the interior plateau, which was thousands of metres in elevation. The road from Vera Cruz to Mexico City was 'improved' several times – in the mid-18th century and again in 1804. Even then, goods were carried by mules rather than wagons. This was far too expensive to make the import or export of farm products profitable, and it conferred a smaller level of protection on local manufacturing as well. Isolation was reinforced by Spanish laws that prohibited trade with any country but Spain and which were intended, like their English counterparts, to reserve the colonial market to Spanish manufacturers.

Almost the only product that Mexico and the Andes could export was silver. As soon as the Spanish had conquered the natives, they searched for precious metals. The biggest discoveries were the Potosi mine in Bolivia (1545) and the Mexican mines in Zacatecas (1545), Guanajuato (1550), and Sombrerete (1558).

Silver had significant disadvantages as the principal export, and they prevented Mexico and the Andes from emulating North American development. First, silver was inflationary. The economies of Peru and Mexico were based on coining money, and the increase in their money supplies pushed prices and wages above world levels. Wheat in Mexico, for instance, was four to ten times as expensive as in Amsterdam. Wages in Mexico were twice those in Italy or India, and wages in the Andes were double Mexican levels. These differentials were sustainable only because of the high cost of transport, Spain's trade restrictions, which kept out cheap imports (although smuggling was an endless problem), and the high cost of Spanish manufacturing itself, which was also inflated by New World silver. Second, silver did not generate many jobs. Mexican silver mines employed 9,143 men in 1597, and Potosi employed 11,000–12,000 in 1603. Employment in the latter declined to 4,959 around 1790. These numbers were negligible compared to the labour forces *in toto* and were much smaller than the numbers involved in producing and supplying the North American farm exports. Third, much of the income generated by silver mining accrued to a small circle of rich owners rather than being disbursed over a broad swathe of the population. Consequently, silver contributed to exceptionally high inequality in Latin America.

Mexico was not a staple economy on the North American model. In 1800, exports amounted to only 4% of GDP. Most of the Mexican economy had nothing to do with exports. Therefore, the distribution of income in Mexico followed laws that were different from the British colonies. In North America, labour and capital were drawn into the colony in response to export opportunities, and their returns were set in England, where the colony had to compete for settlers and investment. In Mexico, wages were determined by internal factors – by coercion of the natives, by the balance of land and labour, and by the efficiency of the economy. The first two were most important in the pre-1650 period of population collapse, while the third was decisive in the subsequent period of population growth.

Before 1650, Mexico exhibited a pattern that is common in many pre-industrial economies: population and wages were inversely related. When the Spanish arrived in the 1520s, the population was very high, and wages were low (Figure 16). Indeed, the power of the *conquistadores* pushed wages even lower than high population implied. As the native population collapsed, the real wage rose (despite attempts to coerce labour) and reached a value of about one in the mid-17th century. At this wage, a full-time worker could support a family at a minimal level of comfort.

After 1650, the Mexican population grew from 1–1.5 million to 6 million in 1800. Over the same period – and this is of great importance – the inverse relationship between population and the wage broke down: the wage rose to twice subsistence even though the population was expanding. The labour supply and the wage could both increase only if the demand for labour was growing faster than the supply. The rise in labour demand reflected rising productivity across the economy. Agriculture was transformed by the integration of European crops and animals (wheat, sheep, cattle) with the indigenous crops (maize, beans, squash, tomatoes, chillies). Transportation was revolutionized with European draught animals (horses and mules). Manufacturing gained impetus through the fabrication of new products (woollen cloth) and the concentration of production in specialized regions that promoted the division of labour. These were the characteristics of English industry that made it more productive than American and precluded manufacturing in the colonies. In contrast, the isolation of Mexico and the Andes and the large size of their populations made manufacturing development feasible. The expansion of the Latin American economy, of course, took place under the sway of Spanish rule and shows that Spain's policies, however illiberal, were not sufficiently detrimental to prevent economic expansion.

While the Mexican economy grew in the colonial period, the society was remarkably unequal. The population was divided into legally defined racial categories, and the divisions corresponded to economic cleavages. One reconstruction shows the Spanish upper class (10% of the population) getting 61% of the total income, while the native peasants (60% of the people) received only 17%. Mexican inequality was greatly in excess of that in the New England and Middle Atlantic colonies and was probably similar to the Caribbean and plantation regions of the US South, although exact measurement is impossible at present. This much inequality proved bad for growth after independence.

Independence: USA

The USA declared independence from Britain in 1776, and its system of government was established, with the Constitution adopted in 1787. The economy took off in the antebellum period (1790–1860). The population increased by a factor of eight, and income per head doubled.

One can interpret the antebellum economy as another example of the staples theory.

Tobacco, rice, and indigo lost momentum, but their place was taken by the greatest staple of them all – cotton. Demand for the fibre soared in Britain as the Industrial Revolution unfolded. Cotton was grown in Georgia but was not a high-profit activity until Eli Whitney invented the cotton gin in 1793. Cultivation then spread across the US South. The crop was grown on large slave plantations, and slave imports expanded until Congress prohibited them in 1808. In the next half century, the slave population grew by natural increase, and the growth was validated economically by the rapid expansion of the cotton textile industry. In the 1850s, cotton was highly profitable, and slavery would not have ended without the Civil War (1861–5).

Staples theorists believe that cotton exports drove the whole US economy. According to this view, Midwestern agriculture expanded in order to supply plantations with food – a conclusion that has been much disputed. Cotton was also responsible for the industrialization of the northeast since southern plantations and western farms were the markets for its products.

The industrialization of the USA also depended on four supportive policies that constituted the 'standard model' for economic development in the 19th century. The first was mass education. Great strides in this direction had been taken in the colonial period, and they were extended in the 19th century and were increasingly guided by economic motives. The other three policies were originally proposed by Alexander Hamilton in his *Report on Manufactures* (1792) and consisted of transportation improvements to expand the market, a national bank to stabilize the currency and insure a supply of credit, and a tariff to protect industry. Without the tariff, the southern and western purchases of manufactures would not have led to US industrialization since Britain would have satisfied the demand, as it did in the colonial period.

Henry Clay, a US senator, dubbed Hamilton's proposals 'the American system', but they were applied by many countries after they were popularized by Friedrich List. The constitution itself was a first step towards implementation since it abolished state tariffs and created the legal basis for a national market. The remaining steps were taken with the construction of the Cumberland road linking the Potomac River to the Ohio River in 1811–18 and the Erie Canal connecting the Hudson River to Lake Erie (1817–25), the chartering of the First and then the Second Banks of the United States in 1791 and 1816, and a series of tariffs beginning in 1816.

Before 1816, the USA had only a low tariff, but the Napoleonic Wars targeted American shipping and led to US protectionist measures, trade embargoes, and a war with Britain in 1812. Manufacturing expanded behind these barriers. After Napoleon's defeat at Waterloo in 1815, the USA enacted the Tariff of 1816 to protect manufacturing, with a duty of 20% on most goods and 25% on textiles. Rates were raised in 1824 and 1828, but high tariffs were controversial and were lowered again in 1846.

Protectionism became a characteristically American policy as Northern interests took charge of the country. The Civil War increased the need for federal revenue, and tariffs were raised with the Morrill Tariff of 1861. Over the next century, tariff rates rose again and again, culminating in the Smoot-Hawley Tariff of 1930. The UK, which had followed free trade since repeal of the Corn Laws in 1846 and the Navigation Acts three years later, enacted a tariff in 1932. Most other countries responded to the world Depression in the same way. It has only been since the Second

World War that the USA has sought to unwind the system of protection, finding that its interests were better served by penetrating other countries' markets than by protecting its own.

US cotton manufacturing grew rapidly behind the tariff wall. In the 1850s, the British industry was the largest in the world, consuming 290,000 tons of raw cotton per year, but the USA was number two (111,000 tons) and considerably ahead of France, which was in third place with 65,000 tons. Alexander Hamilton and Henry Clay would have been pleased that the impetus imparted to the economy by cotton exports had produced such progress.

This conclusion, however, attaches too much importance to staple exports. First, although cotton (and later wheat) were major foreign earners, total exports were only 5–7% of GDP in 1800–60. This was far less than the 30% realized in Pennsylvania and coastal South Carolina, to say nothing of the 41% reached in Jamaica. Cotton and wheat exports were not substantial enough to drive the antebellum economy. Second, the labour market performed better than the staples theory predicts. In the 18th century, the real wage in Pennsylvania was marginally greater than real wages in England, which is what one would expect if the USA was growing and drawing immigrants from Europe (Figure 15). With American independence and European warfare, the Atlantic labour market disintegrated, and the USA real wage grew continuously while British wages stagnated during the Industrial Revolution. By the 1830s, real wages in the USA were double those in Britain. Immigration should have kept wages lower if the staples model was in play.

The rise in GDP and wages indicates that the USA had developed the capacity to generate rising productivity through its own efforts. A major question in staples theory is how and when an economy develops beyond dependence on its staple. Evidently, the USA made the transition in the first half of the 19th century.

A venerable explanation is Habakkuk's hypothesis that the abundance of free land on the frontier generated high real wages – why should anyone work for a low wage in New York or Philadelphia if he could move west and start a farm? – and these, in turn, induced businesses to invent labour-saving technology that pushed up GDP per head and ultimately raised wages even further. The USA, along with Britain and the Netherlands, was one of the handful of economies that consistently pioneered high-productivity, capital-intensive technology in the last two centuries, as discussed in Chapter 4.

Indeed, one can see these forces at work in the cotton textile industry. Its success required the tariff, but the tariff was not enough. The success of cotton textiles depended on technological breakthroughs that produced a particularly labour-saving technology. The high cost of labour led American firms to experiment with machines beginning in the 1770s, but commercial success required workers and managers experienced in the technology. In 1793, the first commercially successful mill was built and managed by Samuel Slater, who had worked in an English factory. The next breakthrough was the construction of an integrated spinning and power weaving mill by the Boston Manufacturing Company in Waltham, Massachusetts, in 1813. Francis Cabot Lowell founded the firm after visiting Britain and seeing power looms, which he sketched from memory. Production models were made by Lowell's engineer, Paul Moody. One of the most remarkable features of the Lowell–Moody system was the degree to which British technology was redesigned to make it suitable to American conditions. By the 1820s, the real wage in America was higher than in Britain, and, as a result, the Americans took up the power loom more rapidly than the British. America was taking the world lead in industrial technology.

American advances were not confined to cotton textiles. In 1782, Oliver Evans built the first automatic flour mill. Before the 19th century, the trigger mechanisms of pistols and rifles were bespoke, and the gunsmith had to fit each component to its companion in order for the mechanism to work smoothly. The Frenchman Honoré Blanc and the American Eli Whitney were the first to conceive and experiment with interchangeable parts, but they could not be made on a mass scale until the milling machine was invented around 1816. American government arsenals in Springfield and Harper's Ferry in the 1820s fabricated interchangeable parts for muskets. American firearms exhibited in the Crystal Palace Exhibition of 1851 so impressed the British that they sent a delegation to study the 'American system'. Interchangeability spread to private arms producers like Colt, then to watch manufacturers in the mid-19th century, and, next, to bicycles, sewing machines, farm machinery, and, finally, automobiles, where they were a building block of Ford's assembly-line system. The success of the American economy depended on the application of inventive engineering across the full spectrum of industries. The incentive to mechanize was provided by the high cost of labour. The successful response required a large pool of potential inventors. The interplay between challenge and response made the USA the world's productivity leader by the First World War.

Independence: Latin America

The Spanish Empire lasted 300 years as an alliance between the monarchy and the white colonial elites. Spain's Bourbon kings tried to create a modern fiscal-military state in the 18th century, but their demands for revenue were resisted in the colonies. Resistance to Madrid, however, was always tempered by the racial and economic divisions in colonial society. The wide-ranging attacks on whites and their property in the Túpac Amaru revolt in Peru in 1780 was only one of many unpleasant reminders of the dangers at the base of the social pyramid. Spanish America had *de facto* independence thrust upon it by Napoleon's invasion of Spain in 1808. Re-establishment of the empire proved impossible. In Mexico, for instance, Miguel Hidalgo led a revolt of natives in

1810 against the ruling *peninsulares* (Spanish-born whites). While this appealed to creoles (Mexican-born whites) at the outset, native violence against whites in general prevented a united movement against Spain, and the revolt was put down. Independence was achieved in 1821 by a creole coup anxious to preserve its privileges, which it saw threatened by rising liberalism in Spain.

Independence brought decades of economic stagnation rooted in the dilemmas of the colonial society. Greater international competition was already undermining Mexico's manufacturing sector in the late 18th century. The result was de-industrialization, as in India. Alexander von Humboldt explained how 'The town of Puebla was formerly celebrated for its fine manufactories of delf ware (*loza*) and hats.' At the 'commencement of the eighteenth century', exports from 'these two branches of industry enlivened the commerce between Acapulco and Peru'. European imports destroyed this trade, however.

> At present there is little or no communication between Puebla
> and Lima, and the delf manufactories have fallen so much off, on
> account of the low price of the stone ware and porcelain of Europe
> imported at Vera Cruz, that of 46 manufactories which were still
> existing in 1793, there were in 1802 only sixteen remaining of delf
> ware, and two of glass.

Real wages slumped from twice subsistence in 1780 to bare-bones subsistence in the 1830s.

The textile industries were also hurt by British imports. Most Mexican cloth was wool, and cottons were imported from Catalonia. When Britain's blockades of Spain in the 1790s cut off imports, cotton cloth production took off in Puebla. The boom was brief, for Spanish imports resumed after 1804, and the country was engulfed with cheap British cloth after independence. The Mexican cotton industry foundered. The response was a version of Henry

Clay's American system and List's proposals for Germany. Lucas Alamán, the Minister of Interior and Foreign Affairs, introduced a tariff on cotton textile imports and channelled some of the proceeds to the Banco de Avío, which financed equipment purchases for new factories. A national market, however, was not created, for state tariffs remained and little was done to improve transportation. Mass education was also ignored.

The results were likewise mixed. On the one hand, about 35 cotton spinning mills were established between 1835 and 1843. Real wages also recovered after 1840. On the other hand, there was no stimulation to an engineering industry since the machines were imported, as were the engineers who installed them and supervised their operation. Moreover, these mills led nowhere. The industry stagnated in the middle of the 19th century, and developments in other industries were meagre. This was no general advance as in the USA.

The next burst of economic growth was during the Porfiriato period under the dictatorship of Porfirio Diaz between 1877 and 1911. He applied the 19th-century development strategy more vigorously than Alamán. A national market was created through an extensive programme of railway building and the abolition of taxes for goods crossing state boundaries. Tariffs were used to support Mexican industries. A policy innovation was to rely on foreign investment, rather than national investment banks, for capital. Foreign investment also became the medium for introducing advanced technology.

Economic development in the Porfiriato was a mixed success. On the one hand, some impressive industrial growth was achieved. GDP per capita rose from $674 in 1870 to $1,707 in 1911. On the other, there was little local contribution to technological progress since foreign engineers simply installed foreign-designed factories, and that absence ultimately meant that development did not spread beyond the state-promoted industries. Moreover, the gains from growth were not distributed widely. Real wages trended downward under Diaz's rule. Revolution broke out in 1911.

Education and invention

Why did the American economy grow so much more rapidly than the Mexican? An influential interpretation attributes US success to the 'high quality' of its institutions and Mexico's performance to the 'low quality' of its. But which institutions? The US advantages ran from an English system of property rights and courts, legislative (and judicial) checks on the executive, egalitarianism (but not in the South), democracy, and *laissez-faire* policies (but not the tariffs). Mexican disadvantages included the natives' communal ownership of land, extreme social and racial inequality, and a political system that perpetuated the worst features of the colonial heritage – a set of courts with conflicting jurisdictions, a state that excessively regulated business, and an inefficient tax system (although one might question their importance in view of the growth achieved in the colonial period).

Economic policies had greater impact on the economy than these institutions. The USA pioneered the standard 19th-century development strategy at the beginning of the century. A national market was created by the Constitution, which abolished state tariffs, and by transportation improvements that were extended as new technologies (steam boats, railways) were invented, a protective tariff was erected in 1816, a national banking system was created to stabilize the currency, and mass education began in the colonial period. Mexico implemented these policies gradually – tariffs and banks in the 1830s, a national market only after 1880, and mass education late in the 20th century. The differences in educational policy go a long way to explaining the different development trajectories.

The different technological trajectories reflect differences in the supply and demand of technology. As early as 1800, real wages in the USA were considerably greater than English wages. This premium created a demand for labour-saving machinery. As invention occurred and productivity rose, wages increased further, and the process became self-reinforcing. In Mexico, on the other hand, wages were much lower, so this incentive was lacking.

The supply of technology was also much greater in the USA than in Mexico. This was not a question of religious differences or of medieval or irrational features of Hispanic culture. We have this on the authority of the great geographer and pillar of German science, Alexander von Humboldt, who lived in Mexico during 1803. He was impressed by Mexican science.

> No city of the new continent, without even excepting those of the United States, can display such great and solid scientific establishments as the capital of Mexico.

He instanced its university, school of mines, art institutes, botanical garden, and savants. The scientific culture was spread to the populace through public lectures, and scientific learning extended far into the provinces.

> A European traveller cannot undoubtedly but be surprised to meet in the interior of the country, on the very borders of California, with young Mexicans who reason on the decomposition of water in the process of amalgamation with free air.

It was not the absence of the Enlightenment that held Mexico back, but a general shortage of skills in the work force. Literacy is an indicator. In the USA, over 70% of adult white males were literate at the end of the 18th century, and close to 100% by 1850. The black slaves (14% of the population), on the other hand, were almost entirely illiterate, so overall literacy for men was about 86%. In Mexico, the white population was also highly literate, and the rest were not: 'the cast of whites is the only one in which we find … anything like intellectual cultivation'. In Mexico, whites comprised only 20% of the population, so the overall literacy rate was of that order.

The technological significance of this difference is clear in the biographies of inventors in the USA and Britain. Virtually all inventors were literate. Illiterate people would have found it difficult to invent since they would have had no access to technical literature. In addition, inventors operated businesses in which they corresponded, entered contracts, obtained patents, and negotiated with clients. To be part of that world, one had to be able to read and write. In the USA, most of the white males were potential members. In Mexico, about 80% of the population was excluded. The scope for a creative engineering response was correspondingly reduced.

The immediate reason for the difference between the two countries is obvious: the USA had more schools than Mexico. New England had achieved close to complete literacy for its male population in the colonial period, with state-financed schools and compulsory attendance. Horace Mann led the renewal of Massachusetts education, and in 1852 a system modelled on Prussia's was adopted. The 'common school movement' spread to other northern states where it met the needs of industry. Mass education became as American as high tariffs. In 1862, the Vermont congressman Justin Smith Morrill, who had sponsored the protective tariff bill the previous year, introduced a bill to grant federal land to states to establish universities. Over 70 so-called 'land grant colleges' were created. Between 1910 and 1940, the 'high school movement' saw the creation of state secondary schools across the country. Since the Second World War, there has been further expansion of high schools and universities.

There was no comparable expansion in education in Mexico before the 20th century. The Revolution led to more schooling, but in 1946 over half of the adults were still illiterate. There has been a great extension of education at all levels in the past half century. For Mexico, however, it came two centuries too late.

Why did the USA and Mexico follow different trajectories? The demand for literacy and numeracy was greater in the colonial USA than in Mexico because the North American colonies were staple economies and the settlers expected to achieve a European standard of living by selling a large proportion of their produce to buy English consumer goods. This commercial activity was facilitated by the ability to read and write. In Mexico, in contrast, the native population was much less commercially active and so found these skills to be less useful.

Governments were also keener to build schools in the USA than in Latin America. The egalitarian economies of New England and the Middle Atlantic states underpinned democratic polities that provided public services like education that were widely demanded. Mexico, in contrast, was run by a white elite whose interests were not served by schooling the masses. So they remained uneducated. Inequality was high, and governments also represented narrow elites in the Andes and in the colonies built on slave labour such as the Caribbean and Brazil, with the same result – little schooling across Latin America.

The USA provides a revealing comparison, for its most prosperous region in the colonial period was also built on slave labour. Why did it not suffer the fate of Jamaica or Brazil? After the abolition of slavery and the end of reconstruction, the states of the South were also highly unequal and governed by an elite that had little interest in educating the African American population. Access to schooling and its quality were low until the end of segregation in the 1960s. This was a major reason why the South became the poorest region of the country. The major difference between the USA and Latin America was the share of the population that was socially excluded. In the USA, African Americans made up one-seventh of the total, while the natives and blacks in Latin

American comprised two-thirds of the total. Had the USA treated 70% of its population as it treated its African Americans, the result would not simply have been injustice on an expanded scale. Rather, it would have been national failure, for the USA could never have become an economic powerhouse with such limited provision of education.

Chapter 7
Africa

African poverty is not new. Sub-Saharan Africa was the poorest region of the world in 1500, and it remains so – despite the increase in income per head that has occurred. The aim of this chapter is to identify the structures and the contingent events that have kept Africa poor for so long.

The 'short list' of candidates is long. Colonial ideology persists in some Western circles, where the poverty of Africans is attributed to their imagined laziness or lack of intelligence. Subtler versions include the view that Africans are bound by tradition or non-commercial values. None of these claims, however, stands up to historical examination.

Institutional explanations for African poverty are also favourites. The slave trade is popular, and, indeed, the poorest countries in Africa today are the ones that exported the most slaves. However, even the countries that resisted the slavers vigorously are still very poor by today's standards, so something else was going on. Colonialism is another favourite explanation since, in many places, its aim was to transfer wealth from Africans to Europeans. While some development occurred under colonial rule, European administration did not kick-start modern economic growth. Dependency theorists say the reason was too much globalization, for they maintain that Africa's concentration on exporting primary products has worked to the continent's disadvantage in the long run. Finally, many recent commentators have emphasized the corruption, interventionism, and authoritarianism of African governments. If failed states were only replaced by Western-run administrations, the economies would take off – but only, of course, if the foreigners got it right the second time around.

To understand why Africa is poor today, we must understand why it was poor in 1500. The answer turns on geography, demography, and the origin of agriculture. The social and economic structure of 1500 then determined how the continent responded to globalization and imperialism, and those responses have kept it poor since.

Africa and the great divergence debate

Sub-Saharan Africa was poor in 1500 because it was not an advanced agrarian civilization. There were only a few – Western Europe, the Middle East, Persia, parts of India, China, and Japan. They were the countries that were in a position to have an industrial revolution. The rest of the world, including Africa, was not, and that is why Africa is left out of the great divergence debate.

The agrarian civilizations had many advantages that set them apart from Africa – productive agriculture, diversified manufacturing, and the institutional and cultural resources necessary for modern economic growth. These included private property in land and landless labourers as well as the cultural correlates needed to organize property and commerce – writing, land surveying, geometry, arithmetic, standardized weights and measures, coins, and a legal system based on written documents and officials who could manage those texts. These cultural elements were necessary for the advancement of trade, for the development of learning, mathematics, and science, and for the invention and diffusion of modern technology. Sub-Saharan Africa lacked these preconditions, as did much of Southeast Asia, Australia, New Zealand, northern Eurasia, Polynesia, and the lightly populated parts of the Americas.

Africa's historical trajectory was influenced by the nature of early agriculture and its relationship to demography. Around 3000 BCE, sheep and cattle were introduced from the Middle East to graze on the Sahara (which was wetter than today), and wheat and barley were grown in the Nile Valley and on the Ethiopian plateau. Later, Ethiopians expanded the plant repertoire by domesticating teff, finger millet, sesame, mustard, ensete, and coffee. Mixed husbandry evolved in which the cropped fields were tilled with ox-drawn ploughs and manured by sheep and cattle. There were also investments in terracing and irrigation. Ethiopia was the only part of sub-Saharan Africa to develop an advanced agrarian civilization. Around 2000–1500 BCE, millet and sorghum were domesticated in the vicinity of Lake Chad. The cultivators also kept sheep, but mixed farming along Ethiopian lines was not practised. Even today, sorghum and millet are cultivated in shifting systems with hoes rather than oxen and ploughs. Finally, yams and palm oil formed the basis of agriculture in the rainforest. Yams were domesticated in Nigeria, where they thrive today. Livestock husbandry was absent since horses, cattle, and sheep died of the sleeping sickness carried by the tsetse fly native to the rainforest.

The farming system of West Africa was responsive to new opportunities as they arose. Between the 1st and 8th centuries CE, new crops were introduced from Asia including bananas, plantains, Asian yams, coco yams (taro), and beans. The repertoire was significantly broadened again in the 16th century with the introduction of maize, manioc (cassava), groundnuts, and tobacco from the Americas. These quickly became 'traditional' crops, showing the vacuousness of 'unchanging tradition' as an explanation of African poverty.

The domestication of crops resulted in permanent farming villages and a rise in the birth rate in Africa as it did everywhere in the world. In the Ethiopian highlands, where tropical diseases were absent, the population grew rapidly. As land became scarce, the state and the aristocracy could support themselves by leasing or taxing it. Communal property was privatized, and landless labourers emerged as people who lost their right to farm wherever they wanted. The Kingdom of D'mt in northern Ethiopia and Eritrea was founded in the 8th century BCE. Its agriculture was based on the plough and irrigation, iron was known, and its language was written. D'mt was succeeded by the grander Kingdom of Aksum.

The growth in population in West Africa was restrained because tropical diseases kept mortality high. The most lethal form of malaria and its associated mosquito (*Plasmodium falciparum* and *Anopheles gambiae*) appeared about the same time that yam cultivators were first clearing the rainforest. These clearings probably contributed to the evolution of the disease. Other tropical diseases such as sleeping sickness also played a role.

West Africa remained a land-abundant farming region, and shifting cultivation was the appropriate response to that circumstance. An example is the group known as the Yakö. They lived in the rainforest of eastern Nigeria and subsisted on yams. In the 1930s, the Yakö village of Umor claimed 40 square miles suitable for cultivation. Only about 3 square miles were planted each year, however. After harvesting, the land was allowed to revert to bush for six years and new land was cleared for planting. Allowing for fallowing, only 21 of the 40 square miles of farmable land were in use. The remainder was available for children or anyone needing land. Consequently, there was no class of landless labourers in the village, nor was there a demand for land to buy or rent since anyone could clear a plot without depriving anyone else.

Table 5. Yakö income, 1930s

Panel A: Food production and consumption			

The family consists of one man, two women, and 3–4 children (4.75 adult equivalents)

The family cultivates 1.4 acres of yams intercropped with pumpkins and okra. Palm oil and palm wine are harvested from wild stands.

food consumption per adult equivalent

	Kg/year	**Kcal/day**	**grams protein/day**
yams	489.2	1582	20.5
cowpeas	12.4	114	8.0
meat	4.4	30	2.4
pumpkins	9.6	7	.2
okra	9.6	8	.5
palm oil	2.1	50	0
palm wine	174.7	150	1.0
total		1941	32.6

Cultivating the yam patch takes 307 days.
The palm products require 93 days.
The meat is purchased.

Panel B: Palm products produced for sale	
palm oil	12 tins @ 36 pounds
palm kernels	747 pounds
palm wine	93 half-gallon bottles

Palm products sold require 155 days of work

Africa

Cultivating yams and harvesting oil and wine from palms did not require much work and provided enough food for subsistence. Table 5, Panel A, shows a reconstruction of the food production of a typical Yakö family in Umor. The family consisted of a man, two wives, and four or five children. Each year, they planted 1.4 acres with yams and some coco yams, with cow peas, pumpkins, okra, and other vegetables planted among them. The diet was overwhelmingly vegetable – a small amount of bush meat was hunted and a bit of purchased meat flavoured the yams. In addition, the family consumed palm oil and half a gallon of palm wine per day. The energy intake amounted to 1,941 calories per adult-male equivalent per day. These people were at bare-bones subsistence. Cultivating their garden and harvesting the palms took the three adults a total of 400 days per year. The consumption pattern of Africans was probably similar before the arrival of the Europeans.

The low population density and high transportation costs limited the possibilities for specialized manufacturers supporting large markets. There was an iron industry, which was established in West Africa around 1200 BCE, but total production was low. Cotton was grown in the savannah and woven into cloth on hand looms. The industry was centred around Kano, but, as with iron, production was at a low level. Instead of buying manufactures, most people made their own simple implements and bark clothing. Consequently, the range of available consumer goods was limited. People grew enough food to meet their own needs but nothing more, since there was nothing to buy with the surplus. Cultivation took only part of the year, and for the rest they enjoyed leisure.

Two styles of politics were attractive with this production system. The first was the band or tribe – a confederation of the cultivators in an area. It could organize the allocation of land and resolve disputes about its use, and the men constituted a militia that defended the territory from other groups. Leaders were styled 'chiefs' and held their posts through persuasion. This political system was relatively egalitarian.

Shifting cultivation included one feature that gave rise to hierarchical social organization, and that feature was the large amount of leisure enjoyed by cultivators. If they were compelled to work more, they would grow food beyond their subsistence requirements, and that surplus could support complete idleness for some or (at the political level) a military establishment. The attractions of idleness and power made slavery compelling. The difficulty was that an empty landscape presented slaves with opportunities to run away and support themselves. The French Congo furnishes 20th-century examples: villagers fled into the bush and lived for years as foragers to avoid military conscription or forced labour on rubber plantations. African chiefs eliminated this option by slave-raiding in other regions, so captives did not know the local language or how to survive in the local ecology. Of course, their children knew these things, so slavery often lasted only one generation, and the children of slaves were admitted as members of the tribe. Slavery was common in Africa before the Europeans arrived and was the basis of many states.

While Africa had states, they were different from states in advanced agricultural economies. Agrarian states could support themselves through taxing land or renting out state property. That was not possible in Africa since land was so abundant as to be worthless. As a result, African states lacked the legal and cultural institutions that advanced agricultural societies used to organize private property such as surveying, arithmetic, geometry, and writing. The exceptions that prove the rule were the West African empires of the Savannah like Ghana, Mali, and Songhai. Farmland was communally owned, and slavery was widespread. State revenue, however, came mainly from taxing trans-Saharan trade and gold production (not agriculture). Islam was adopted in these empires, and contributed writing and property law to solve their administrative problems.

The slave trade

The arrival of Europeans led to profound changes in societies practising shifting cultivation, for the Europeans introduced a far broader range of goods than the natives possessed. It never took long for aboriginal Americans, Polynesians, or Africans to realize that cotton made better clothing than bark or that guns were more deadly than spears. In 1895, Mary Kingsley trekked through Gabon and reported that most Africans,

> young and old, men and women, regard trade as the great affair
> of life, take to it as soon as they can toddle, and don't even leave it
> off at death, according to their own accounts of the way the spirits
> of distinguished traders will dabble and interfere in market matters.

Africa was not unique in this regard. Before the French arrived, the Huron of Canada cooked in a hollowed-out stump filled with water brought to the boil with hot stones. The natives were so impressed by the kettles of the French fur traders that they imagined that the man who made the biggest pots must be the King of France. To buy the European kettles, axes, and cloth, the natives needed something to sell in return, and when they found their staple, they increased their working year to produce it for export. In North America, the product was fur. In c.1680, a Micmac joked with a French Franciscan:

> In truth, my brother, the Beaver does everything to perfection. He
> makes for us kettles, axes, swords, knives, and gives us drink and
> food without the trouble of cultivating the ground.

West Africa exported gold to the Mediterranean and Arab worlds, but a far more important export emerged in the 16th century – slaves. The sugar economy of the Americas generated a great demand for labour that could be satisfied most cheaply by buying workers. In 1526, Alfonso I, the African King of Kongo who sought to convert his people to Christianity, complained to the Portuguese King João III that 'many of our subjects eagerly lust after Portuguese merchandise that your subjects have brought to our domains. To satisfy this inordinate appetite, they seize many of our free black subjects … [and] sell them' to slave traders on the coast. In the 17th century, kingdoms like Dahomey and the Ashanti, which had long been based on slavery, responded to the external demand for slaves with warfare and raiding. The captives were marched to the coast where they were sold to European ships. The African kings used the proceeds to buy firearms (which increased their power and helped their slave-raiding), textiles, and alcohol. Between 1500 and 1850, 10 to 12 million slaves were transported to the New World. Millions more were taken across the Sahara, or over the Red Sea and Indian Ocean for sale in Asia.

Legitimate commerce

In the 18th century, enlightened and religious opinion turned against slavery, and the trade was abolished in the British Empire in 1807. Slaves were replaced with new exports – the so-called 'legitimate commerce'. The first new product was palm oil, which was in demand as a lubricant for machinery and railway equipment as well as to make soap and candles. In 1842, Francis Swanzy, an English magistrate on the Gold Coast, told a British parliamentary committee how the new export trades increased the work effort of Africans by providing them with the opportunity to purchase consumer goods:

> The wants of the people are daily increasing. Go into the native's house and you will find articles of European furniture; in his house European implements of agriculture; they wear more clothes; in fact, their situation is greatly improving, their wants increasing, and they cannot supply those wants basking idly in the sun; they must work.

Cotton cloth amounted to over half of Britain's exports to West Africa, and metals and metal products including firearms accounted for much of the rest. Asked how they could afford British products, Swanzy replied:

They go into the bush and dig for gold; a great many make palm-oil. There was 20 years ago, scarcely any exported; now there is a great deal exported; ground nuts also are exported.

The oil was transported to the coast along the same commercial networks that had previously moved slaves. Nigeria was the largest exporter, but production spread throughout West Africa. The commercial possibilities were enlarged further in the middle of the 19th century, when it was discovered that the kernel of the palm fruit yielded an oil well suited to margarine. Palm oil could be raised on plantations, but it remained the domain of individuals harvesting wild stands. In Nigeria in the early 20th century, for instance, 2.4 million hectares of wild groves were harvested, as opposed to 72,000 hectares in estate plantations and 97,000 hectares planted by smallholders. The typical Yakö family discussed previously worked an extra 155 days per year to produce 12 four-gallon tins (each weighing 36 pounds) of palm oil, over 700 pounds of palm kernels, and 93 half-gallon bottles of palm wine sold locally. Their biggest purchases were cloth and clothing, but they also bought cutlery, utensils, cosmetics, ornaments (all imported), and meat.

Since the reason Africans produced palm oil was to buy European goods, their incentive depended on how much cloth they could get for each can of oil that they sold. Figure 17 shows the price of palm oil relative to cotton cloth at West African ports from 1817 to the present. In the case of palm oil, there was a sharp rise in the price of oil relative to cloth from 1817 to the middle of the 19th century. Africans could get more and more cloth for their oil over this period, and that induced them to increase production. British imports rose from a few tons per year in 1800 to 25,000 in the middle of the 19th century to almost 100,000 tons around the First World War.

Palm products were not the only West African exports. Cocoa was another great success. The bean was indigenous to the Americas and introduced into Africa in the 19th century. In Britain, the price of cocoa doubled with respect to the price of cotton cloth between

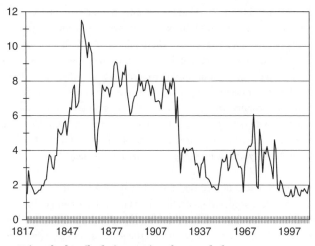

17. Price of palm oil relative to price of cotton cloth

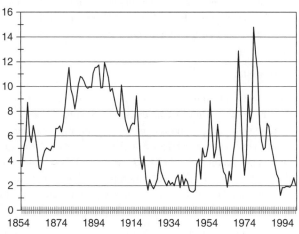

18. Price of cocoa relative to price of cotton cloth

the 1840s and the 1880s (Figure 18), and that increase prompted Africans (not Europeans!) to experiment with its production, which began on a large scale in Ghana in the 1890s. Since cocoa was not indigenous, forest had to be cleared and trees planted. This posed a challenge to communal property systems, which let any tribal member occupy empty land. The Africans modified their system of property to facilitate cocoa growing. One solution was to separate ownership of the trees from ownership of the land, so that the planter of the tree secured a return on his investment whoever was growing yams or manioc in the surrounding fields.

A more radical solution was effected by the Krobo. Groups of Krobo collectively purchased land from other tribes and then divided it amongst themselves in individual tenure. Once they had developed their plots, they repeated the process, moving westward across Ghana eventually into the Côte d'Ivoire. As a result, many Krobo own plots scattered across these countries. Some plots they farm, and some they lease out. Migration and homesteading required a high level of investment that was financed with savings from cocoa trees already in production. The Krobo look like Weber's Protestant ethic in operation.

Colonialism

European colonialism began with the Portuguese, who established settlements in what are now Guinea-Bissau, Angola, and Mozambique in the 15th and 16th centuries. The other leading European powers established forts on the coast of West Africa to facilitate slave trading, and the Dutch established their settlement on the Cape of Good Hope in 1652. European colonialism became more earnest in the 19th century, but it was not until the end of the century that the continent was divided among the imperial powers.

Colonies were acquired for economic as well as strategic reasons. The hope was that they would supply tropical products to the imperial power and be a market for its manufactures, as well as providing places for its citizens to settle and profitable investments for its bourgeoisie. In addition, empires were regarded as civilizing missions that would spread Christianity and raise native culture to the standard of Europe. These aims were expected to be accomplished at no cost to the imperial power, since colonial governments were supposed to finance their expenditures with their own revenues.

Colonialism proved even more detrimental to economic development in Africa than in other parts of the world. African colonialism created remarkably bad institutions. The early African colonies, like their predecessors in North America, were organized through 'direct rule', in which the colonial government applied metropolitan law throughout its territory to settlers and natives, although the latter were often non-enfranchised. By the late 19th century, however, direct rule was replaced by 'indirect rule'. The aim was to make foreign occupation palatable to the indigenous population by recognizing every ethnic distinction and by offering power and wealth to compliant leaders in exchange for supporting the foreigners. In this system, the colonial state applied metropolitan law to settlers and in cities. Control of the natives in the countryside was devolved to 'chiefs' who applied the 'customs' of their 'tribe'. The terms are in quotes to emphasize that they were legal concepts of the colonial state with little necessary connection to the pre-colonial reality. All African polities, from kingdoms like the Ashanti to the least structured band, were conceived as equivalent entities with uniform customs, despite the fact that the complex polities included conquered peoples with disparate customs. Chiefs were created in places like northern Ghana and eastern Nigeria where they had never ruled before. Many of the polities had been fluid, and the right of people to leave oppressive regimes was a check on tyrannical rulers. This right was removed when people were assigned to tribes they could no longer leave. Custom was redefined to suit colonial purposes. 'Barbaric' customs like slavery were eliminated (although it continued in practice), while useful customs like a chief's right to demand unpaid labour were retained. In that way, forced labour became a normal feature of colonial life. Communal landownership usually became a custom, so people could acquire farm land only by being members of a tribe – and at the discretion of the chief, to whom they were subservient. Traditional processes were used where possible to ennoble chiefs, but, in the final analysis, they were appointed by the occupying power. Chiefs were given more authority than rulers had before colonialism. The new-style chiefs became the foremen of empire, levying taxes, compelling labour, and using their powers to amass personal fortunes. Colonialism created a system of rent-seeking petty despots to rule the countryside.

The policies pursued by African colonies were at least as detrimental to growth as those followed in India and elsewhere. Colonial governments adopted only one element of the standard 19th-century development model – transportation improvements. By the First World War, 35,000 kilometres of railway were opened in sub-Saharan Africa. These were financed by private investment (often with public guarantees) and were intended to facilitate exporting primary products by linking the interior to ports. Tariffs were not used to promote manufacture but were kept at low levels for revenue purposes only. The colonial economies were, therefore, fully integrated into the world market. As ocean freight rates declined and overland transport costs fell, the prices of European manufactures declined in Africa and the prices of primary products increased. The economies reacted accordingly. The production and export of products like palm oil and ground nuts shot up; conversely, the production of cotton textiles in Kano declined. Globalization meant that the economy of Africa became specialized in the production of primary products.

Colonial governments did not attempt to educate the African population. The task was left to Christian missions, Muslim madrasahs, and other independent initiatives. Some progress was made, particularly among groups like the Krobo, whose commercial activities gave them an incentive to acquire literacy and whose success gave them the income to purchase schooling. Literacy rates remained very low until after independence. Colonial governments also made no effort to establish local banks to finance investment. Some colonies did promote foreign investment, but it was at the expense of Africans, for the foreigners were granted ownership of the continent's resources. There were considerable differences between colonies in this regard.

At one extreme were the British colonies in West Africa. They were the birthplace of indirect rule, and exemplified it most perfectly. Most of the country was under the control of the chiefs. The acquisition of land by Europeans was discouraged: William Lever, for instance, was denied large land concessions to establish oil palm plantations in Nigeria in 1907.

The German, Belgian, and French colonies in West Africa adopted land and labour policies that were less favourable to native interests. Land was expropriated by colonial governments and given to European investors for plantation and mining development. The Belgians permitted Unilever to establish oil palm plantations in the Congo, for instance. Africans were conscripted to work on plantations and build railways.

At the opposite pole from the British West African colonies were the settler colonies. South Africa is the most extreme example, but the history of land expropriation was similar in Zimbabwe and the Kenyan highlands.

The Cape Town colony had about 25,000 Dutch, German, and Huguenot settlers when it was taken over by the British in 1806. The European population grew to 100,000 in 1850 and leapt to one million in 1900 following the discovery of diamonds in 1866 and gold in 1886. The African population probably rose from 1.5 million to 3.5 million between 1800 and 1900. After 1835, the Boers advanced out of the Cape colony into the Transvaal, seizing vast quantities of land from the Africans. The Boers established the

Orange Free State and the South African Republic, which were incorporated into South Africa after they were conquered by the British in the war of 1899–1902. The British were no more sympathetic to African land rights than were the Boers. The culmination of the land seizures was the Natives' Land Act of 1913, which made it illegal for the Africans to buy or lease land outside of the native reserves. These amounted to 7% of the land of South Africa, even though Africans made up two-thirds of the population.

Parallel but less extreme distributions obtained in other settler colonies. In Zimbabwe, for instance, when the Fast Track Land Reform Programme started in 2000, 4,500 white farmers owned 11.2 million hectares of the country's best land, while one million African families lived on 16.4 million hectares of poorer-quality communal land. Under these circumstances, the law of real property is a system that protects privilege rather than a system that encourages everyone to advance their interests by making mutually advantageous trades.

Dispossessing the natives from the land was a policy to secure their labour as well as to acquire their land. The Reverend J. E. Casalis observed in the 1860s that the aim of land seizures was:

> to force the natives ... to live within such narrow limits that it
> becomes impossible to subsist on the produce of agriculture and
> livestock and to be compelled to offer their services to the farmers
> in the capacity of domestic servants and labourers.

This objective was extended by the labour-control systems of apartheid, which treated Africans as though they resided in the reserves and were merely guest workers in the country at large.

Contemporary poverty in historical perspective

Early in the 19th century, West Africa embarked on a trajectory that had much in common with the colonies of North America – the economy was export-oriented, the Africans pushed back the rainforest in response to high prices in global markets, and income was ploughed back into businesses. All this enterprise and progress, however, failed to spark off modern economic growth. Why not?

There are immediate explanations and underlying causes. The immediate explanation is contained in Figures 17 and 18. They show that the real prices of palm oil and cocoa have trended downwards since the early 20th century. Both prices fell during the First World War and reached extremely low values during the 1930s and the Second World War. The price of palm oil (relative to cloth) never recovered its pre-First World War value, and today is lower than it was in the 1930s. Cocoa-producing countries have fared better – but not cocoa growers. World market prices trended erratically upwards after the Second World War and hit peaks higher than those of the

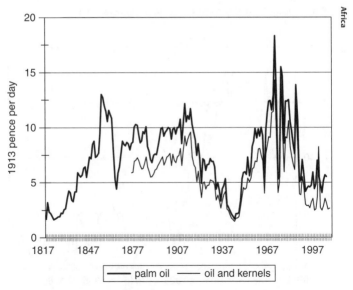

19. Earnings per day from palm oil

1890s. In the principal cocoa exporters like Ghana, the increases in income accrued to the state rather than the farmers, however, because the growers were forced to sell their cocoa to a state-owned marketing board that resold the product internationally. Ostensibly, the marketing board protected the growers from fluctuations in the world market by paying steady prices, but in reality the boards acted like Soviet procurement agencies and creamed off the rising surplus from international sales. By keeping prices low, the marketing boards reduced the incentive to expand production, as well as keeping the rural population poor.

The price history translates directly into the real income of the farmers. Figure 19 shows the combined real earnings per day of a hypothetical Yakö family harvesting both palm oil and kernels. The figure is constructed on the assumption that their efficiency did not change over the period – the actual state of affairs. The earnings from palm oil followed the same rollercoaster as its price. Since 1980, the real incomes of palm producers have been as low

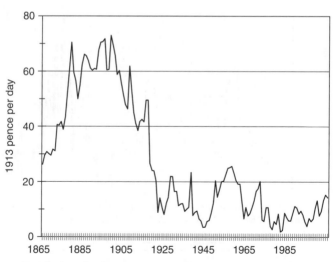

20. **Earnings per day from cocoa**

as they ever were in the 1930s. Cocoa producers have seen a similar long-run drop, but they missed the rising incomes of the 1960s and 1970s since the cocoa marketing board did not pass the high world market prices on to the growers (Figure 20).

Today, cocoa producers earn about 10 pence per day in 1913 purchasing power. This was the wage of a labourer in Accra at that time. Palm oil producers earn half as much. The situation is the same with all of Africa's agricultural exports. Since agriculture employs about 60% of the population, earnings in that sector determine earnings throughout the economy. The reason that Africans are poor is because the continent's agriculture generates a First World War standard of living.

There are two reasons why African agriculture does not do better. The first is the fall in the price of farm exports. There are three reasons for this. One is the invention and cheapening of substitute products. The advent of the petroleum industry in the second half of the 19th century resulted in better and less expensive lubricants than palm oil. Paraffin, another petroleum product, ousted the palm oil derivative stearine from candle-making, and, of course, candles themselves were superseded by kerosene lamps and then by electric lights. The second is competition with Asian producers. Oil palms were cultivated in large plantations in Sumatra and Malaya in the early 20th century, and the plants grew better than in West Africa. Since the Second World War, Malaysian and Indonesian exports have dominated world markets and forced down the prices received by Africans. The third reason for low prices is the expansion of production in Africa itself. This factor is particularly important for cocoa since most production is still African, and there are no good substitutes for cocoa in chocolate manufacturing. Cultivation of cocoa expanded westward across Ghana into the Côte d'Ivoire. The work force was drawn from impoverished regions across West Africa. Output has increased, and prices have fallen. From this perspective, African poverty is a vicious circle in which low wages keep down export prices, and low prices keep down wages.

The second reason that cocoa and palm oil do not generate higher incomes is because productivity is low and stagnant. In part, the story is biological. The Germans and the Belgians undertook basic research on the oil palm, but, ironically, the benefits have been realized in Southeast Asia to the detriment of Africa. Compared to other continents, there has been very little research to improve African crops.

Mechanization is another source of productivity growth. Most of the labour in producing palm oil is expended in processing the fruit once it is picked. The traditional method involves stacking, fermenting, boiling, pounding, treading, soaking, skimming, and pressing. Sticks are used for pounding, the feet for treading, and so forth. Great strides have been made in mechanizing the processing of fruit grown on plantations, but progress has been lethargic in the village sector. Simple machines for pressing the fruit and expelling the oil considerably reduce the need for labour but at the cost of more capital. These machines are not profitable on small farms in West Africa due to the low wage rate. This is an example of the technology trap discussed in Chapter 4 whereby low wages mean that it is not profitable to adopt the mechanized technology required to raise wages. In any event, there is little point in freeing labour from processing palm oil since the non-agricultural population already exceeds the number of jobs outside of agriculture.

This labour market imbalance reflects developments of the last 50 years. One has been the growth in population, which has increased five-fold since 1950. A definitive explanation is impossible in view of the limited African data, but the experience of other tropical regions suggests that the immediate cause was a fall in mortality rates, particularly for infants and the elderly. Very likely, this was due to improvements in public health and the spread of modern medical practices.

The other development has been the failure of Africa to industrialize in this period. There are economic explanations for this as well as broader institutional explanations. All of them make sense in terms of Africa's geography and history.

There are three economic explanations for the lack of industry. The first is comparative advantage. North America exported wheat to Europe since wheat production is land-intensive and the USA had abundant land relative to its population. Africa has an even lower population density than North America, so its comparative advantage lies in commodities that use its land and resources intensively. These are the primary products it exports. In the USA, the counterpart to land abundance was high wages, which would have made manufacturing uncompetitive with imports in the 19th century had there been no tariffs. The situation is different in Africa, however, for wages are low, yet manufacturing firms still do not find it profitable to locate there. The reason is, presumably, that costs would be high since production would be inefficient. One reason for low productivity might be uneducated workers, but education has expanded rapidly in recent decades, so any deficit in that area among young workers has disappeared – without any noticeable benefit.

Another reason for low productivity is the absence of other complementary firms. In rich countries, production takes place in urban networks where firms support each other by providing specialized products and services. These 'external economies of scale' raise productivity and allow firms to pay high wages while remaining competitive. Africa is caught in a vicious circle – a network of firms will never be established since no firm finds it profitable to set up business in the absence of the network! In the 19th century, Africa may have had the beginnings of these networks with its scattered iron works, the textile industry at Kano, and so forth, but globalization, supported by colonialism, drove them out of business.

A final economic argument is technological and applies the analysis of agricultural mechanization to the industrial sector: wages in Africa are too low to make it profitable to use the highly capital-intensive technology of modern industry. Africa is caught in yet one more trap: mechanized industry is the solution to low wages, but low wages make mechanization unprofitable!

The most popular explanations for African poverty, however, are institutional rather than economic: one aspect of 'bad institutions' is endemic warfare, which surely is bad for business. Poverty itself is a cause of warfare since it makes recruiting troops very cheap. Low wages causing war, which, in turn, restrains the economy, leading to low wages – another poverty trap. In addition, the actors and issues in many well-known wars were the creations of colonial indirect rule. Belgium controlled Rwanda by elaborating the difference between Tutsi and Hutu into an imaginary racial division. The Tutsi were conceived as foreign interlopers, who were superior since they were descendants of the biblical character Ham, while the Hutus were regarded as indigenous and inferior. The colonial administration lavished education and opportunities on the Tutsi, so that they could rule the Hutu. However, the Hutu majority finally seized control of the state in the revolution of 1959. When a Tutsi army invaded the country in 1990 and defeated the predominantly Hutu Rwandan army, the Tutsi threatened the gains made by Hutus since 1959, and the stage was set for the genocide.

Another aspect of 'bad institutions' is the corruption and undemocratic character of many states. These deficiencies are also legacies of colonial structures of government. Newly independent African states inherited constitutions that included racial distinctions and embedded the tribal and administrative structures of indirect rule. The states have been successful in eliminating racism but much less successful in eliminating tribalism. In most countries, there are separate systems of administration for urban and rural areas. The former have modern systems of law, and the latter are divided into the 'tribal' areas created during the colonial period and run by chiefs administering colonial customs including communal landownership. Often, the continuation of colonial administration is obscured by adopting uniform legal codes that cobble together the modern and the customary rules in the same document. Much of rural Africa is consequently governed by a layer of non-elected corrupt potentates who can extort income and labour services from the citizenry and extract rents from the national administration.

The goal of economic development has added another dimension to the control of the peasantry. The ideology of the 1960s (both Western and Communist) saw development as a process in which the urban economy grew at the expense of the rural. The colonial state had used the system of indirect rule to govern the countryside for the benefit of the colonial power. The leaders of independent states took their place and used the same techniques to benefit the city at the expense of the countryside. Chiefs were induced to use their 'traditional' ownership of communal land to expropriate it for development projects, threats of eviction were used to compel peasants to cooperate with agricultural innovations, and rural residents were coerced to labour on infrastructure and plantation projects. In addition, the state directly coerced peasants; in particular, farmers were forced to sell crops to government marketing boards, so that food could be sold cheaply to urban workers and export crops could be taxed by paying the peasants low prices for products that were sold in international markets at high prices, as we have seen in the case of cocoa. These efforts brought little industrial development, while reducing agricultural incentives and increasing corruption and authoritarianism.

Radical and Marxist-Leninist states followed a seemingly different path but with similar outcomes. These states abolished tribalism as well as racism: in the words of Samora Machel, the first president of Mozambique: 'For the nation to live, the tribe must die.' One-party states were created to suppress divisions and as vanguards of progress. The practice of colonialism, however, was harder to change. Tribal leaders became cadres of the ruling party and carried on as before. In the name of development, the reformed states adopted the dirigisme of colonial administration – forced labour re-emerged in them as well. Africa cannot easily escape its history.

Chapter 8
The standard model and late industrialization

By 1850, Europe and North America had pulled ahead of the rest of the world. How the poor countries could catch up was the new problem. Colonies could do little, since their options were restricted by the imperial power. Independent states, however, could apply the standard model – railways, tariffs, banks, and schools – that had worked for the USA and Western Europe. This strategy, however, proved less and less fruitful as time went by.

Imperial Russia

Russia was for a long time the most backward part of Europe. Peter the Great (1672–1725) tried to turn it into a modern Western power. He built the new port of St Petersburg and founded many factories mainly devoted to the military. There was no catch-up with the West, however. The extent of Russia's backwardness was made clear by the country's defeat by England and France in the Crimean War (1853–6). Modernization was so pressing that Tsar Alexander II abolished serfdom. Reformers hoped this would kick-start economic growth by creating free labour and private property, but there was no quick response.

The post-emancipation government adopted the standard development model with some modification. First, a national market was created through a vast programme of railway construction. By 1913, 71,000 kilometres of track were open and linked Russia to the global economy.

> When the peasants marketed their grain in Nikolayev [in 1903], they asked, 'What is the price in America according to the latest telegram?' And what is still more surprising they know how to convert cents per bushel into kopecks per pood.

Second, tariffs were used to build up industry. By 1910, Russia smelted 4 million tons of pig iron per year. It was not in the first division with the USA, Germany, and the UK, but it was a leader in the second. Russia also developed an important engineering industry. In addition, the state promoted light industry with high tariffs on cotton textiles and moderate tariffs on raw cotton. As a result, the cultivation of cotton expanded in what became Uzbekistan. In the early 20th century, Russian mills processed almost as much cotton as Germany's. Third, the biggest innovation in economic policy lay in finance. Private banks were too weak to play the role they had in Belgium or Germany. Instead, Russia relied on foreign capital. Railways were financed by selling securities abroad, and foreign direct investment became the principal means of bringing advanced technology to the country. Plants were built to West European specifications, however, without any adaptation to Russia's different economic circumstances, with the result that production costs were higher than in Western Europe. Fourth, education was expanded from the 1860s onwards. By the First World War, almost half of the adult population was literate. Even amongst manual workers, the earnings of the literate were higher than those of the illiterate, so schooling was attractive to many people.

The standard model (as amended) boosted the share of heavy industry in Russia from 2% of GDP in 1885 to 8% in 1913, but agriculture remained the biggest sector (its share slipped from 59% to 51%). Agricultural output doubled over this period as the world price of wheat rose, and farming accounted for most of the growth in GDP. Tsarist economic growth was mainly an agricultural boom, souped up with some tariff-induced industrialization. Growth would probably have petered out when the world price of wheat collapsed after the First World War. Another economic model was needed to catch up to the West.

An indicator of the limited impact of the standard model in Russia was the state of the labour market. Despite the growth in GDP, labour demand did not grow enough to fully employ the population, so wages remained at subsistence, and the extra income created by growth accrued as profits to the owners of industry and as rent to the owners of land. These became the flash-points of social conflict. Unequal development led to a revolt in 1905 and, more explosively, in 1917. The failure of the standard model to transform Russia led to its own undoing.

Japan

Japan is a particularly interesting case, for it was the first Asian country to catch up with the West. Japanese history is divided into four periods: Tokugawa (1603–1868), when the country was governed by Tokugawa shoguns; Meiji (1868–1905), when power was returned to the Emperor Meiji and economic modernization began; Imperial (1905–40), when heavy industries were founded; and, finally, the Era of High Speed Growth (1950–90), when Japan caught up with the rich countries of the West.

The roots of Japan's success lie in the Tokugawa period, although the country had many institutions that were inimical to economic growth. Society was divided into castes – samurai, peasants, artisans, and merchants – and the polity into several hundred domains ruled by lords called daimyo. Domains could be confiscated, and this created insecurity of property at the highest social level – rather like Elizabethan England. Draconian restrictions were imposed on international trade and contacts.

Inbound ships were only allowed from China, Korea, and the Netherlands, and the Dutch were restricted to a tiny settlement in Nagasaki.

Technology advanced in the Tokugawa period, but the character of the improvements was the reverse of Britain's. Since wages were low in East Asia, the Japanese invented technology that increased the employment of labour in order to raise the productivity of land, capital, and materials. Labour, for instance, was deployed constructing irrigation systems to raise crop yields. New varieties of rice such as *akamai* were planted, and water control allowed a second crop such as wheat, cotton, sugar cane, mulberry, or rapeseed to be grown. Farmers worked more hours per hectare and used less capital, as hoes were substituted for ploughs and draft animals.

Productivity in manufacturing processes was also improved. Domains tried to attract industries and supported research to raise their productivity since more production led to more tax revenue. In the case of silk, early experiments to use machinery along English lines (for example, employing gear and belt systems inspired by clocks and automatons) were abandoned since they were not economic. Instead, experiments were directed at improving the productivity of silk worms. Selective breeding and temperature control cut maturation time and boosted silk per cocoon by one-quarter. In mining, mechanical systems of drainage were known but not used; instead, armies of workers did the work. Likewise, much labour was expended to extract the maximum amount of metal from ores. The exception that proves the rule was sake. Capital-intensive, water-powered factories were installed but only because the government restricted production by limiting the time during which breweries could operate. That restriction led to high-volume plant design.

Tokugawa development produced uneven prosperity. The population and rice crop both grew in the 17th century, but the wages of labourers stayed at 'bare-bones' subsistence. The average person consumed about 1,800 calories per day in the late Tokugawa and early Meiji periods. Most calories and protein came from rice, potatoes, and beans rather than meat or fish. The correlate was that people were short: men averaged 157 cm and women 146 cm.

Many people, nonetheless, enjoyed a more affluent lifestyle. About 15% of the population lived in cities; Edo (modern-day Tokyo), with a population of one million, Osaka, and Kyoto (each 400,000) were amongst the largest cities in the world. Life expectancy was increasing. Leisure grew as peasants took 'recreation days' and travelled around the country. School attendance was very high for an agrarian society. In 1868, 43% of boys and 10% of girls attended school, where they learned reading and arithmetic. More than half of adult men were literate. Reading for instruction and pleasure was widespread. Books were too expensive for most people to buy, but they could be rented from shops. In 1808, there were 656 rental bookshops in Edo, supplying about 100,000 households (roughly half the population) with books. The high level of education was probably due to the commercialization of the Japanese economy, and it underlay later growth.

Tokugawa Japan achieved an impressive level of engineering and administrative competence that was apparent in the establishment of the first iron foundry in Nagasaki. Military necessity was the impetus. In 1808, *HMS Phaeton* entered the city's port to attack Dutch shipping. *Phaeton* threatened to bombard the harbour unless provisions were provided. The Japanese had no iron cannon to defend themselves since they had no furnaces to cast them. Nabeshima Naomasa, who became the lord ruling Nagasaki and who was an enthusiast for Western science, established a team to create a cannon foundry. The group included savants and craftsmen skilled in iron. They translated a Dutch book describing a foundry in Leyden and replicated it. In 1850, they succeeded in building a reverberatory furnace, and three years later were casting cannon. In 1854, the Nagasaki group imported state-of-the-art, breech-loading Armstrong guns from Britain and manufactured copies. By 1868, Japan had eleven furnaces casting iron.

The Meiji Restoration

In 1839, the British attacked China to force the country to allow the importation of opium, which was one of the East India Company's most lucrative products. Narco-imperialism triumphed with China's defeat in 1842. Would Japan be next? The answer seemed to be 'yes' when the US Commodore Perry arrived with four warships in 1853 and demanded that Japan end its restrictions on foreign trade. Without a modern navy, Japan felt it had to agree and signed treaties with the USA, Britain, France, and Russia. An adequate military was urgent. The Tokugawa shogun took some steps to improve Japanese security, but many regarded this as too little, too late.

In 1867, the Emperor Meiji ascended the thrown. Modernizers effected a virtual *coup d'état*, and the last Tokugawa shogun relinquished his powers. The slogan of the modernizers was 'rich country, strong army'.

The new regime undertook sweeping reforms. All of the feudal domains were 'surrendered' to the Emperor, and the 1.9 million samurai were paid off with government bonds. The four orders of society were abolished, so anyone could take any job. The peasants were confirmed in the ownership of their land and modern property rights were created. Feudal payments were replaced by a land tax to the national government. This provided most state income in the 1870s. In 1873, universal conscription was introduced and a Western-style army created. This further eroded the privileges of the samurai, who had previously been the only people allowed to bear arms. In 1890, a written constitution that created a constitutional monarch on the Prussian model was adopted.

The radical spirit of Meiji Japan is shown by a simple problem – the measurement of time. The traditional Japanese clock divided the interval from sunrise to sunset into six hours and from sunset to sunrise into another six hours. The day hour and the night hour, therefore, differed in duration, and, moreover, the length of each varied over the course of the year. Tokugawa clockmakers experimented with ingenious modifications of Western mechanical clocks to reproduce these hours. In 1873, the first Japanese railway was completed, and the Meiji government faced the problem of publishing a timetable. Rather than a complicated schedule with departure and arrival times varying over the year, the state instead abolished traditional Japanese time and replaced it with the Western 24-hour clock. Modern transportation required modern time.

Meiji economic development

The Meiji government would have liked to develop the country with the standard model that had been successful in Western Europe and North America, but they could easily introduce only two of its four components. The first was the creation of a national market by abolishing the tariffs between domains and building a railway network. The second was universal education. In 1872, elementary schooling was made compulsory, and, by 1900, 90% of the school-age children were enrolled. Secondary schools and universities were founded but were limited and highly competitive. Thousands of Japanese were sent abroad to study. As a result, education progressed much earlier in Japan than in other poor countries. Table 6 contrasts Japan with Indonesia, a country whose experience is representative of most of Asia and Africa. In Japan, a high proportion of the population (10.8%) was in school by the late 19th century, and modern levels of participation (19.7%) were reached by the Second World War. Indonesia, by contrast, lagged several generations behind Japan. Mass education was an important reason for Japan's success in adopting modern technology.

Table 6. Percentage of the population in school

	Japan	Indonesia
1870	2.5	0.1
1880	6.7	0.1
1900	10.8	0.4
1913	14.1	1.1
1928	17.5	2.8
1940	19.7	3.4
1950	22.3	7.0
1973	17.2	13.6
1989	18.8	23.9

The other components of the development model – investment banks and a protective tariff – were harder to implement. Tokugawa Japan had nothing like modern banks. The Meiji state chartered banks from the outset, but the system was chaotic. It took 50 years for Japan to develop a banking system along German lines. Early in the Meiji period, the state filled the gap by acting as the venture capitalist.

It was impossible for Japan to use tariffs to promote industrial development because the maximum tariff rate was capped at 5% by a treaty forced on Japan by the Western powers in 1866. Instead, the state intervened directly in the economy through 'targeted industrial policy'. The most important actors were the Ministries of the Interior and Industry, which were charged with importing modern technology. The Ministry of Industry established Japan's railway and telegraph systems in the 1870s and

1880s. Foreign technicians initially guided the project, but a school to train Japanese engineers was established in Osaka, and the foreigners were dispensed with as quickly as possible. One reason the Japanese managed the projects was to ensure that procurement policy promoted Japanese industry. Japanese potters, for instance, received contracts to make insulators for telegraph lines, and, in that way, an industrial ceramics industry was created.

In the 1870s and 1880s, both ministries operated on the assumption that Japanese business would not introduce modern technology at the required pace, so that the state had to be the entrepreneur. State-owned mines and factories were established using advanced imported machinery, but most were commercial failures. The Tomioka silk-reeling factory, for instance, was built in 1872 with French machinery and steam power but always lost money. In the 1880s, the Japanese government sold most of its industrial establishments and relied on business to make management decisions within the framework established by the state. Japanese business solved the problem of importing technology by re-engineering it to make it appropriate for Japanese conditions.

Japan faced a problem that has only become worse with time: modern technology was embodied in machinery and plant specifications that were designed for Western firms facing Western conditions. By the late 19th century, wages were much higher in the West than they were in Japan, so Western designs used much capital and raw materials to economize on labour. This configuration was inappropriate for Japan and resulted in high costs. Some countries limped along with inappropriate technology, but the Japanese response was far more creative: they redesigned Western technology to make it cost-effective in their low-wage economy.

Silk-reeling was an early example. At the same time that the Tomioka mill was losing money, the Ono merchant family in Tsukiji established a mill that also used European-inspired machinery. In this case, however, the machines were made of wood rather than metal and the power came from men turning cranks rather than a steam engine. The modification of Western technology along these lines became common in Japan as the 'Suwa method'. This was an appropriate technology for Japan in that it used less expensive capital and more cheap labour.

It was the same story with cotton. The early attempts to spin with mules were not successful. Much more successful was the *garabô* (rattling spindle) invented by Gaun Tokimune. The *garabô* could be produced cheaply by local carpenters (so it saved capital) and produced yarn similar to that produced by hand wheels with which it was competing. The *garabô* was not a high-level Meiji project, but it was supported by the Association for Developing Production run by Gaun's local prefecture.

The contrast with India is telling. The cotton-spinning industry that grew rapidly in Bombay in the 1870s used English mules, and the mills were operated in the same manner as in Britain. No systematic attempts were made to reduce capital in the Indian industry. Such efforts were made in Japan, however. An elementary step was to operate the mills with two eleven-hour shifts per day rather than one, which was normal in Britain and India. This cut capital per hour worked in half. From the 1890s onwards, high-speed ring spindles were installed instead of mules. These changes in technique all increased employment relative to capital and cut costs. By the 20th century, Japan was the world's low-cost spinner of cotton and was out-competing the Indians and Chinese as well as the British.

Development of appropriate technology extended to agriculture. The Japanese experimented with US farm machinery in the 1870s, but it was unsuccessful because it used too much capital. More successful were efforts to increase the productivity of land, even if that required the use of more labour. In 1877, *shinriki* rice was developed near Osaka. It gave high yields if it was fertilized and if the paddy was thoroughly tilled. Veteran farmers' organizations were enlisted by the Ministry of Agriculture to spread this culture to the rest of the country. Agricultural output grew steadily in Meiji Japan and made an important contribution to the growth of the economy – once invention focused on increasing the productivity of land, the scarce and expensive factor of production.

The Imperial period, 1905–40

While Japanese society was overhauled in the Meiji period, change in the economic structure was slow. The leading industries were traditional – tea, silk, and cotton. Exports of these products paid for imported machinery and raw materials.

Industrial growth accelerated between 1905 and 1940, and its character changed. The share of manufacturing leapt from 20% of GDP in 1910 to 35% in 1938. The metallurgical, engineering, and chemical industries that dominated post-war Japanese growth were founded in this period, as were the famous firms that produce these products.

These advances coincided with the full implementation of the standard development model. Japan recovered control over its tariffs in 1894 and 1911, and they were immediately raised to protect industry. By the 1920s, the banking system had matured to the point that it could finance industrial development. In addition, Japan retained its system of targeted industrial policy. The combination of policy instruments proved particularly potent for promoting heavy industry.

The first step was taken in 1905 when the Yawata Steel Works were established for strategic reasons. The plant was state-owned and required subsidies for years before becoming profitable. The First World War gave a boost to Japanese business since European imports were cut off. After the war, the military undertook research in conjunction with private companies, and promoted key industries like automobiles, trucks, and aircraft with procurement contracts. Large-scale firms, along with banks that financed them, were owned by holding companies. These *zaibatsu* coordinated production and channelled investment to industry.

While the *zaibatsu* aimed to deal with the shortage of capital in Japan by increasing the rates of savings and investment, management also responded to the factor prices it faced by inventing appropriate technology. American firms operating in a high-wage environment invented highly mechanized, assembly-line production systems that economized on labour. Japanese firms, in contrast, economized on raw materials and capital. One of Japan's most famous products was the Mitsubishi Zero fighter. Its maximum speed of 500 kilometres per hour at 4,000 metres was not achieved by increasing the power of its engine but instead by reducing its weight. One expedient developed in the 1930s was 'just in time' production. Rather than producing components for inventories that required capital to finance, Japanese businesses produced components only as they were needed. 'Just in time' production is a technique that has proved to be so productive that it is now used in settings where capital is cheap as well as where it is dear.

Unlike Tsarist Russia or Mexico, foreign investment was a comparatively unimportant channel for importing Western technology. Instead, Japanese firms established their own R&D departments to copy it and re-engineer it to suit Japanese conditions. Business was supported by the state. When it proved impossible to import electrical turbines from Germany in 1914, Hitachi was awarded a contract for a 10,000-horsepower turbine for a hydro-electric project. Since the largest turbine Hitachi had previously built was 100-horsepower, there was much to learn, and the experience strengthened the firm's engineering capabilities.

Japan's application of the standard development model was a mixed success. On the one hand, an urban society with advanced industries was created. Per capita GDP increased from $737 in 1870 to $2,874 in 1940. Given the stagnation that gripped most of the Third World, these achievements were impressive. On the other hand, the rate of growth in per capita income (2.0% per year) was modest and not much above the US rate of 1.5%. If these rates had continued after 1950, it would have taken Japan 327 years to catch up to the USA. That was not fast enough.

The slow growth of the economy was reflected in weaknesses in the labour market, as in Russia and Mexico. The large-scale firms paid high wages, but wages remained very low in agriculture and small-scale industry because labour demand was weak. These sectors continued to use hand technology or only simple machines. There was a symbiosis between the modern and traditional sectors: if a stage in a modern production process could be performed least expensively by small-scale, handicraft methods, then it was subcontracted to a small firm.

Latin America

Latin America has undertaken the most recent experiments with the standard model. These began at the same time as the southern part of the continent was integrated into the world economy.

Mexico, the Andes, Brazil, and the Caribbean had been part of the world economy since the 16th century, but southern Latin America was too far from Europe for trade to be viable. After 1860, efficient steamships made it profitable to export wheat from Argentina and Uruguay, and guano and copper from the Pacific coast of the continent. Meat exports were added to the list in 1877, when the first refrigerated ship, *Le Frigorifique*, carried frozen mutton from Buenos Aires to Rouen. Exports boomed, and the region attracted settlers and capital from Europe. By

1900, the southern cone was one of the richest regions in the world, and Argentina joined Mexico in developing manufacturing.

Many Latin American countries were too small to become industrial nations and continued to export primary products and import manufactures – and continued to be poor. The larger economies, on the other hand, experimented with the standard development model in the late 19th century and persevered with it until the 1980s, when it was dubbed 'import substitution industrialization' (ISI). First, 90,000 kilometres of railways were laid in Argentina, Brazil, Mexico, and Chile by 1913. Second, tariffs protected industries like textiles and iron. Third, the Russian model was followed with investment financed abroad. Fourth, a notable lapse, however, was the failure to provide universal education. Argentina was the great exception, for it mandated compulsory, free schooling in 1884. As a result, Argentina (followed closely by Chile) led the continent, with over half its adult population literate in 1900 – compared to one-quarter in Mexico, Venezuela, and Brazil.

Manufacturing development gathered pace behind tariffs in the 1920s and 1930s, and the low prices of the continent's agricultural exports lent weight to arguments for industrial development. This sentiment was turned into doctrine by the UN Economic Commission on Latin America, under the direction of the Argentine economist Raul Prebish. *The Economic Development of Latin America and its Principal Problems* (1950) contended that the prices of the primary products exported by Latin America were falling with respect to the prices of the manufactured imports and recommended state promotion of industry to counter the trend. This so-called 'dependency theory' has been politically influential, although its claims are debatable. Consider examples in this book. The history of palm oil and cocoa are in accord with the theory since their prices have fallen with respect to the price of cotton cloth since the mid-19th century (Figures 17 and 18).

However, the price of raw cotton *rose* with respect to the price of cloth in India in the 19th century, leading to de-industrialization (Figures 12 and 13).

Dependency theory led to a comprehensive application of the standard model. Education was finally made universal. Development banks were created to fund development, while foreign investment became the vehicle for financing industry and introducing advanced technology. Tariffs and government controls were used to promote a range of modern industries. Manufacturing output and urbanization soared. Per capita income more than doubled between 1950 and 1980. Foreign debt grew as well, however, and could no longer be serviced when interest rates rose in the early 1980s. Mexico defaulted in 1982, Western banks called in loans, and Latin America went into recession. The standard model had reached its limits.

The failure of tariff-induced industrialization also reflected deeper factors like the evolution of technology. The difference in wages between rich and poor countries had grown, so that the new highly capital intensive technology of the 1950s was even less suitable to poor countries than was the technology of 1850. In addition, a new problem appeared. The new technology of the mid-20th century involved not only high capital to labour ratios but also large plant sizes. These were often too big for the markets of poor countries.

Automobiles are an important example. Most Latin American countries promoted their production, but markets were too small for efficient operation. The MES (minimum efficient size) for vehicle assembly plants in the 1960s was 200,000 autos per year. The MES for engines and transmissions was closer to one million per year, while sheet metal presses could produce four million units in their lifetime. Only seven companies (GM, Ford, Chrysler, Renault, VW, Fiat, and Toyota) produced at least one million autos per year and had engine, transmission, and assembly plants of MES. (Efficiency in metal stamping was realized by changing body design only every few years.) Smaller firms were burdened with higher costs.

Latin American car markets were smaller. In the 1950s, about 50,000 new cars were sold each year in Argentina. The Automotive Decree of 1959 required that 90% of the content of vehicles sold in the country be manufactured there. Production grew at 24% per year until 1965, when 195,000 vehicles were produced, and automobiles accounted for 10% of the economy. ISI looked a great success in terms of the growth in output, but the industry was far too small to realize the economies of large-scale production. The small size of the national market was exacerbated by its division amongst 13 firms, the largest of which produced only 57,000 vehicles. The upshot was that the cost of producing an automobile in Argentina was 2.5 times the cost in the USA. Argentina could never compete internationally with this industrial structure, and the overall efficiency of the economy was dragged down by this sector. Since the same story was repeated in steel, petrochemicals, and other industries, ISI played a big role in depressing GDP per worker and, hence, the standard of living.

The contrast with the 19th century is stark. Scale was not an issue then. Around 1850, a typical cotton mill had 2,000 spindles and processed 50 tons of yarn per year. The USA consumed about 100,000 tons of yarn annually, so it could accommodate 2,000 cotton mills of the MES. It was the same story in other modern industries: a blast furnace produced 5,000 tons per year and total consumption in the USA was about 800,000 tons, or 160 times MES; a rail mill rolled 15,000 tons of rails per year, while the USA laid 400,000 tons (only 27 times more!). The high USA and European tariffs raised the prices paid by consumers in the 19th century, but they did not burden their economies with an inefficient industrial structure. That is a fundamental reason why the standard model worked in North America but not in South America.

The end of the standard model

In Tsarist Russia, Japan, and Latin America, the standard model generated modest economic growth, but not enough to close the gap with the West. With per capita GDP growing at about 2% per year in the advanced countries, poor countries had to generate at least that much growth just to stay even and very much more to catch up in a short time-frame. Tsarist Russia, Japan, and Latin America could not do that with the standard model. A corollary was the slow growth of labour demand that fell short of the growth in population. As a result, Tsarist Russia and Latin America suffered from high inequality and political instability. Many groups in pre-Second World War Japan – workers in agriculture and small-scale industry and women generally – likewise failed to share in the growth. These problems have worsened with time as the scale of efficient production has increased and capital to labour ratios have become even greater in rich countries. Even without the financial crisis of the early 1980s, the standard model had reached the end of its useful life. What would replace it?

Chapter 9
Big Push industrialization

The West pulled further ahead of most of the rest of the world in the 20th century, but some countries bucked the trend and caught up, notably, Japan, Taiwan, South Korea, and (less completely) the Soviet Union. China looks on course to do the same. Growth in these countries was very rapid, and the gap was closed in half a century. They began their growth spurts with an income per head equal to only 20–25% of that in the advanced countries. With the latter growing at 2% per year, the poor country could catch up in two generations (60 years) only if its per capita GDP grew at 4.3% per year. This requires total GDP to grow at 6% or more per year depending on population growth. That is a high hurdle. The only way large countries have been able to grow so fast is by constructing all of the elements of an advanced economy – steel mills, power plants, vehicle factories, cities, and so on – simultaneously. This is *Big Push* industrialization. It raises difficult problems since everything is built ahead of supply and demand. The steel mills are built before the auto factories that will use their rolled sheets. The auto plants are built before the steel they will fabricate is available and, indeed, before there is effective demand for their products. Every investment depends on faith that the complementary investments will materialize. The success of the grand design requires a planning authority to coordinate the activities and ensure that they are carried out. The large economies that have broken out of poverty in the 20th century have managed to do this, although they varied considerably in their planning apparatus.

Soviet economic development

The Soviet Union is the classic example of a Big Push. The 1917 Revolution was followed by four years of civil war, which was won by the Bolsheviks, who conceded the peasants' demands for ownership of the land and its equal division among the farming population. By 1928, the New Economic Policy had revived the economy, Lenin was dead, and Stalin was in power.

The USSR faced the same problem as other poor countries: most of the population was in the countryside engaged in handicraft production and small-scale agriculture. The country needed to build a modern, urban economy. That, in turn, required massive investment in modern technology. The Soviet solution was central planning, and the Five Year Plan became its symbol. Since Soviet businesses were state-owned, they could be directed with instructions from the top (the plan) instead of following the incentives of the market. For a long time, the Soviet model looked like a great success and inspired planned development in many poor countries.

The Soviet Big Push began with the first Five Year Plan in 1928. The growth strategy rested on four legs. The first was channelling investment into heavy industry and machinery production. This accelerated the capacity to build capital equipment and thereby pushed up the rate of investment. The USSR was large enough to absorb the output of large-scale factories, which became the norm. The second was the use of demanding output targets to direct business operations. Since maximizing output might lead to losses, bank credit was liberally given to businesses so that they could cover their costs. The 'hard budget constraints' of capitalism were replaced by 'soft budget constraints'. Third, agriculture was collectivized. Politically, this was the most controversial policy since it was anathema to the peasants, who preferred small family farms and periodic redistributions of land by the village to ensure equality. In the event, collectivization resulted in a huge fall in farm output and led to famine in 1933. The fourth was mass education. Schooling was quickly made universal and compulsory. Adult education was pursued vigorously to cut the time for the whole labour force to be trained.

These measures caused the economy to grow rapidly. By the time the Germans invaded in 1940, thousands of factories, dams, and power plants had been built. The plans tilted investment to heavy industry, which boomed. By 1940, pig iron production had increased from a pre-war maximum of 4 million tons per year to 15 million tons. This was twice as much as Britain produced, but still only half as much as the USA. Electric power generation went from 5 to 42 billion kilowatt-hours. (Lenin once quipped that Communism meant 'Soviet power plus the electrification of the whole country'. By that definition, the Revolution was a success.) The investment rate rose from about 8% of GDP in 1928 to 19% in 1939.

The production of consumer products also increased but by a smaller amount. Partly, this reflected priorities; partly, it was due to the disastrous collectivization of agriculture. Production rebounded by the end of the decade, however. In 1939, the USSR processed about 900,000 tons of ginned cotton. This was double the 1913 level, 50% more than Great Britain (whose output had fallen considerably due to Japanese competition), but only 52% of the USA's. While per capita consumption fell sharply in 1932 and 1933, there was a 20% rise in average living standards between 1928 and 1939. In addition, educational and health services were enormously extended.

The Second World War was a huge blow to the USSR: 15% of the Soviet citizens lost their lives (mortality among men aged 20–49

reached 40%), and housing and factories were destroyed.
However, the capital stock was restored by 1950, and rapid
economic growth resumed. Investment was kept at about 38% of
GDP. By 1975, the USSR produced more than 100 million tons of
pig iron and had surpassed the USA. Consumer goods output also
increased rapidly. It looked like the Soviet model might really be
the best way for a poor country to develop.

And then it all went wrong. The growth rate gradually declined
in the 1970s and 1980s. By the end of the decade, it was nil.
President Gorbachev called for 'restructuring' (*perestroika*).
Central planning gave way to the market, but it was too late to
save the USSR, and it was dissolved.

In the case of the Soviet Union, there are really two questions.
First, what went right? Why did the GDP per head grow so rapidly
from 1928 to the 1970s? Part of the answer relates to 'GDP' and
part to 'heads'. GDP grew rapidly since Soviet institutions were
effective in building large-scale, modern factories. Channelling
investment into heavy industry increased the capacity to build
structures and equipment, and soft budget constraints created
jobs for people who would otherwise have been unemployed in a
surplus labour economy. Even the collectivization of agriculture
made a contribution (although a small one) by accelerating the
migration of people to the cities where the new jobs lay. At the
outset, planning did not require much vision since the object was
to fit Western technology to Russian geography.

The second reason that GDP per head grew rapidly was because
population growth was slow. The number of people rose from 155
million in 1920 to 290 million in 1990. In part, slow growth was
due to excess mortality from collectivization and, especially, the
Second World War, but their importance was dwarfed by the
decline in the fertility rate. In the 1920s, the average Soviet
woman had seven children. By the 1960s, this had dropped to
2.5. The growth in urbanization made a contribution,

but the most important cause in the USSR (as in poor countries generally) was the education of women and their paid employment outside the home.

Second, what went wrong? Why did growth slow in the 1970s and 1980s? The possible answers range from the transient to the fundamental and include the end of the surplus labour economy, the squandering of investment on Siberian development, the arms race with the USA which drained R&D resources from civilian industry, the increased difficulty of planning once technological catch-up was completed and the task was to design the future, the impossibility of central control (what would happen to the US economy if the president had to manage it?), and the cynicism and conformity bred by dictatorship. The collapse of the Soviet Union led many observers to reject state planning and celebrate the virtues of the free market. However, other countries did better with alternative forms of planning.

Japan

The aims of Japanese policy before the Second World War were summarized in the slogan 'rich country, strong army'. Defeat in the war led Japan to reject the 'strong army', but it pursued 'rich country' with even greater commitment. Japan needed a Big Push to close the income gap with the West. The project was remarkably successful. Per capita income grew at 5.9% per year between 1950 and 1990, with a peak rate of 8% between 1953 and 1973. By 1990, West European living standards had been achieved.

Japan accomplished this advance by reversing the technology policy that it had pursued in the Meiji and Imperial periods. Instead of adjusting modern technology to its factor prices, Japan adopted the most modern, capital-intensive technology on a vast scale. The investment rate reached about one-third of national income in the 1970s. The capital stock grew so rapidly that a high-wage economy was created within a generation. Factor prices adjusted to the new technological environment, rather than the other way around.

Japanese industrialization in the post-war period required planning, and the key agency was the Ministry of International Trade and Industry (MITI). The policy tools that Japan had perfected in the 1920s and 1930s were used to accelerate the growth rate.

MITI concerned itself with two kinds of problems. One related to the scale of production – the issue that defeated ISI in Latin America. Steel was one of Japan's great successes. Production had increased from 2.4 million tons in 1932 to a peak of 7.7 million tons in 1943, then dropped to 0.5 million in 1945, and had returned to 4.8 million in 1950. A key feature of steel production is that costs are minimized with large-scale, capital-intensive mills. In 1950, minimum efficient size was 1–2.5 million tons. Most US mills were bigger than that, but only one Japanese mill (Yawata, with a capacity of 1.8 million tons) was in the range. The rest of Japan's mills produced half a million tons or less. As a result, Japanese steel was at least 50% more expensive than US or European steel, despite Japan's low wages. MITI's objective in the 1950s was to restructure Japan's industry so that all steel was produced in mills of efficient size. MITI's power came from its control of the banking system and its authority to allocate foreign exchange, which was needed to import coking coal and iron ore. By 1960, capacity had grown to 22 million tons in modernized, large-scale mills. After 1960, MITI's guidance was less direct. Expansion continued through the construction of new facilities on 'green field' sites. These were all of minimum efficient size, which had by then increased to about 7 million tons; in contrast, most capacity in the USA was in old mills of less than efficient size. Japanese mills were also technically more advanced. 83% of Japan's steel in the mid-1970s was smelted in basic oxygen furnaces against 62% in the USA, and 35% was continuously cast compared to 11% in the USA. Despite a large increase in wages, Japan was the world's low-cost steel producer due to its commitment to modern capital-intensive technology. Over 100 million tons were produced in 1975.

Who was going to buy all that steel? Shipbuilding, automobiles, machinery, and construction were major domestic purchasers. Those industries had to expand in step with the steel industry. Ensuring that result was a second planning problem. Their technologies also had to be decided, and a large-scale, capital-intensive approach was taken with these as with steel. In the case of automobiles, for instance, Japanese firms had more capital per worker than their US counterparts, and the Japanese capital was more effective since 'just in time' delivery meant that much less of it consisted of unfinished components. Also, the scale of production was larger in Japan. In the 1950s, the minimum efficient size of assembly plants was close to 200,000 vehicles per year. Ford, Chrysler, and General Motors annually produced 150,000–200,000 vehicles per plant. In the 1960s, new Japanese auto plants incorporated on site stamping and multiple assembly lines to push the minimum efficient size above 400,000 units per year. All Japanese manufacturers produced at this level, and the most efficient, like Honda and Toyota, could reach 800,000 vehicles per plant per year. Japan's move to highly capital-intensive methods created the most efficient industry in the world, and one which could price its products competitively and still pay high wages.

A third planning problem was to ensure an expansion of consumer demand in Japan to purchase these consumer durables. Japan's distinctive industrial relations institutions made a contribution: among large firms, company unions, seniority wages, and lifetime employment meant that some of the surplus of successful firms was shared with their employees. Small firms, however, provided many jobs in Japan, and in the 1950s (as in the interwar period), they paid low wages. During the 1960s and

1970s, the vast expansion of industry ended the labour surplus, and the dual economy disappeared, as wages in the small firm sector rose rapidly. Rising incomes from the expansion of employment led to a revolution in lifestyle as Japanese bought refrigerators and automobiles made with the enlarged supply of steel. Not only did the Japanese have more gadgets, but they ate better and grew taller. In 1891, the average conscript was 157 cm tall, while his counterpart in 1976 was 168 cm. Japanese consumer spending validated the decisions to expand capacity and raise wages, so that the capital-intensive technology was appropriate – after the fact, if not before.

A final planning problem related to the international market. This problem had ramifications far beyond MITI. In the mid-1970s, the Japanese steel industry was exporting almost one-third of its output, mainly to the USA. Similar percentages of automobiles and consumer durables were also shipped there. The US production of steel and autos collapsed under the impact of Japanese competition; indeed, the decline of the American Rust Belt was the counterpart to Japan's Economic Miracle. The USA could easily have prevented these imports by continuing the high tariff policy it had followed since 1816. So-called 'voluntary export restraints' were negotiated, but they were only temporary expedients. Instead, the USA elected to cut tariffs but only if other countries did likewise (multilateral trade liberalization). One reason was that the USA emerged from the Second World War as the world's most competitive economy, so expanding its export opportunities seemed more rewarding than unnecessarily protecting its home market. Japan's export success called this assumption into question. Japan, however, had established itself as the USA's bulwark against Communism in East Asia, and its geopolitical importance maintained its trade options.

The era of high-speed growth could not last forever. The end of the boom is conventionally dated to the collapse of the real estate and share bubbles in 1991, which ushered in an era of deflation.

The cause, however, was more fundamental, for it was the elimination of the conditions that allowed rapid growth in the first place. Japan grew rapidly by closing three gaps with the West – in capital per worker, education per worker, and productivity. This was done by 1990, and Japan was then like any other advanced country: it could grow only as fast as the world's technology frontier expanded – a per cent or two each year. The post-1990 growth slowdown was inevitable.

China

South Korea and Taiwan have followed close on Japan's heels in catching up to the West. Both were Japanese colonies, which gave them an ambiguous start. Modern educational systems were created, but the emphasis was on teaching Japanese rather than Korean or Taiwanese. Infrastructure and agricultural development aimed to make the colonies food suppliers for Japan. Per capita income reached $1,548 in 1940. Following the Second World War, the Japanese were expelled, their property seized, and their land holdings redistributed among the rural population, creating egalitarian peasant societies. Beginning in the 1950s, both countries vigorously pursued industrialization. South Korea, in particular, followed the Japanese Big Push model closely. Advanced technology was imported and mastered by Korean firms since foreign firms were excluded from the country. The state planned investment and restricted imports to protect the Korean manufacturers it promoted. As in Japan, high quality and performance were advanced by requiring these firms to export large fractions of their production. Korea established the heavy industries like steel, shipbuilding, and autos that were Japan's successes, and, a decade or two later, they became Korea's successes as well.

The rise of South Korea and Taiwan is impressive but will be dwarfed in significance if China continues to industrialize as rapidly as it has in recent decades. When the Communists seized power in 1949, GDP per capita was at rock bottom ($448). By 2006, income reached $6,048 per head, placing China among the middle-income countries. This was far better performance than most of Asia, Africa, or Latin America (Table 1).

How did China do it? The usual answer is 'free-market reforms', but this is incomplete. The economic history of China since 1949 divides into two periods – the planning period (1950–78) and the reform period (1978 to present). In the first, China adopted a Communist system with collective farms, state-owned industry, and central planning along Soviet lines. The development strategy favoured the expansion of heavy industry to create the machinery and structures of an urban, industrial society. The investment rate was pushed to about one-third of GDP, and industrial output grew rapidly. Technology policy, dubbed 'walking on two legs', combined capital-intensive, advanced technology with labour-intensive manufacturing where feasible. Steel production, always an objective of Big Push industrializers, jumped from about 1 million tons per year in 1950 to 32 million in 1978. Despite gyrations in policy, including the Great Leap Forward (1958–60), the subsequent famine, and the Cultural Revolution (1967–9), per capita income more than doubled from $448 in 1950 to $978 in 1978 (2.8% per year). This was no mean achievement but did not distinguish China from many other poor countries.

Following Mao's death in 1976, Deng Xiaoping began 'reforms' in 1978. Planning has been dismantled and a market economy created in its stead. Unlike Eastern Europe's 'shock therapy', China has reformed by gradually modifying and supplementing its institutions. Since 1978, growth has also surged.

The first reforms were in agriculture and illustrate the complexity of the issues. Two reforms were particularly important: First, in 1979 and 1981, state procurement agencies increased their purchase prices by a total of 40–50% for production beyond the obligatory deliveries specified in the plan. Second, collective cultivation was replaced by the Household Responsibility System. Under the HRS, the land of the collectives was divided into small farms leased to families, who were obliged to deliver their share of the commune's plan obligations but who were allowed to keep the income from sales at the high prices for production that exceeded quotas.

Farm output surged as these policies were put in place, and that is the main case for their importance. Between 1970 and 1978, GDP originating in agriculture grew at 4.9% per year, which is even more than the 3.9% realized between 1985 and 2000. However, between 1978 and 1984, output leapt up at 8.8% per year. Grain production also grew faster in 1978–84 than it did before or after. Since the rise in prices and the HRS increased the financial incentive for peasants to increase output, the usual conclusion is that the policy changes caused the output growth.

Reform, however, has to share the credit with other developments that were consequences of earlier planning decisions. The reason that Chinese farmers could increase output was because they could use advanced technology that was also coming together at the same time as rural institutions were reformed. Increasing grain yields requires three improvements under Chinese conditions – better water control, high-yielding seed, and fertilizer. There was a large increase in irrigated acreage in China between the 1950s and 1970s, and millions of tube wells were drilled in north China to supply water there. The increase in the supply of water contributed to the growth in grain output during the planning period, and was a prerequisite for the rapid output growth around 1980.

Dramatic yield increases required seed that responded to fertilizer. The biological problem is a general one in the tropics: if fertilizer is applied to the traditional varieties of rice, they produce more leaves and longer stalks. The plant eventually topples over (lodges), preventing the formation of grain. The solution lies in dwarf rice with fibrous stalks that do not lodge, so that the extra growth from fertilizing goes into seed rather than foliage. Japanese rice was naturally of this character, which was the biological basis for the growth in farm output in the Meiji period. Japanese rice could not be cultivated further south, however, due to differences in the length of the day, so it was necessary to breed dwarf varieties suitable to tropical latitudes. The most famous is IR-8, which was developed at the International Rice Research Institute in the Philippines and released in 1966. IR-8 and its successors have been the basis of the Green Revolution in much of Asia. What is less well appreciated is that China got there first. The Chinese Academy of Sciences' breeding programme produced a high-yield dwarf rice two years before IR-8. It was the diffusion of the new dwarf rice that caused Chinese farm output to explode.

High-yielding rice gives high yields only if it is heavily fertilized. In the 1970s, Chinese farmers were already using traditional fertilizers to the maximum. Heavier application required the industrial production of nitrate. Efforts to increase fertilizer production in the 1960s had not been particularly successful, so in 1973–4 the state purchased 13 ammonia factories from foreign suppliers. These came on stream in the late 1970s and provided the fertilizer that caused yields to shoot up. There is no way to know whether the rise in farm output between 1978 and 1984 required the reforms or whether it would have occurred anyway.

The character of technological change in Chinese agriculture resembles that of Japan and reflects the development of technology tailored to the country's factor proportions. As in Japan, labour was abundant and land scarce, so technological advance has until recently concentrated on augmenting the productivity of land. Comparatively little investment has been directed towards saving labour. The history of the Green Revolution in China differs in this respect from its history in India, where mechanization accompanied the adoption of high-yielding crops. Access to cheaper credit gave large-scale farmers the advantage in India, and they increased the size of their holdings at the expense of small farmers, who often lost their land. Farm machinery allowed fewer people to cultivate the soil. China avoided these conflicts. The communal ownership of land equalized holdings in China and preserved small farms, which was a more rational response to the abundance of labour and scarcity of capital, as well as being more equitable.

Reforms have also transformed the industrial sector. The first steps were also taken in the countryside. Manufacturing by-employments had always been a feature of rural China and were taken up by collective farms. After 1978, 'township and village enterprises' (TVEs) were promoted by local party officials. Consumer goods production had lagged, and the TVEs filled the gap, selling their goods in the free market. The consumer goods industries had low capital to labour ratios (unlike the heavy industries that were the focus of planning), so the TVEs used appropriate technology for China, which is why they succeeded in market competition. Between 1978 and 1996, TVE employment grew from 28 million to 135 million, and TVEs increased their share of GDP from 6% to 26%. Marketization was extended throughout the state sector from the mid-1980s when the state froze its plan targets and allowed enterprises to sell production beyond plan requirements on the free market. Since then, the economy has 'outgrown the plan' and become increasingly market-driven, as it has expanded.

In 1992, the 14th Party Congress endorsed the 'socialist market economy' as the goal of reform, and material balance planning, the centrepiece of central planning, was abolished. Subsequent reforms created a financial system to take the place of state allocation of investment and converted state-owned enterprises from government departments into publicly owned corporations. The reform of state-owned industry has involved deep cuts in employment and closing down unproductive capacity. This is a result that the USSR never accomplished and which may have contributed to its growth slowdown by locking a large share of the work force in unproductive jobs rather than redeploying them to new, high-productivity facilities. As investment has become more market-driven, the investment rate has remained high. The state remains active, if less formally involved, in guiding investment in energy and heavy industry. Perhaps for this reason, the steel industry has continued to grow explosively. It now produces 500 million tons per year. The USA, the USSR, and Japan never produced more than 150 million tons, so China has broken all world records. China's population is, of course, much larger, but production per head, now 377 kg (up from 2 kg per head in 1950 and 102 kg as recently as 2001), has reached the consumption level of rich countries. Between 1978 and 2006, per capita income grew at 6.7% per year.

The reforms are the usual explanation for the high growth rate. As with agriculture, the explanation is incomplete. China's 'reformed institutions' may have improved the country's performance compared to Mao's system, but they have not produced superior institutions to those found in most poor countries of the world; indeed, were China growing slowly, its slow growth would be blamed on the property rights, legal system, and Communist dictatorship that it now has. The crucial comparative question about China is not 'why have China's mediocre market institutions performed better than central planning?', but rather 'why have its mediocre market institutions worked as well as they have?' The answer may come down to legacies from the planning period or other features of China's society or its policies that distinguish it from poor countries generally.

Legacies from the planning period have certainly played a role. These include a highly educated population, a large industrial sector, low mortality and fertility rates, and, despite the Cultural Revolution, a scientific establishment with significant R&D capabilities. Primary education was expanded throughout the planning period, with the result that two-thirds of the population

144

were literate according to the 1982 census, and vocational skills were also widespread. Life expectancy had increased from less than 30 years in the 1930s to 41 in the 1950s, to 60 in the 1970s. (It reached 70 in 2000.) The average number of children born to the average woman (the total fertility rate) dropped from over 6 in the 1950s to 2.7 in the late 1970s – even before the one child policy in 1980. As in the USSR, low fertility was probably the result of educating women and giving them the chance to earn money in paid employment.

However historians ultimately factor out the importance of the planning legacy, reformed institutions, sensible policy, and supportive culture, China is completing a historical cycle. If the country grows as rapidly in the next three decades as it has since 1978, it will close the gap with the West. China will become the world's biggest manufacturing nation just as it was before the voyages of Christopher Columbus and Vasco da Gama. The world will have come full circle.

Epilogue

China is on course to catch up with the West, but what of Africa, Latin America, and the rest of Asia? Income per head in the rich countries grows at about 2% per year, so countries must grow faster than that to close the gap. Many poor countries in Asia and Latin America would have to grow at 4.3% per person per year to catch up to the rich countries in 60 years. For that to happen, total GDP would have to grow at least 6% per year for 60 years. Much poorer countries, like many in sub-Saharan Africa, would have to grow even faster, or it would take even longer to catch up.

Very few countries have sustained such rapid growth over a long period. Between 1955 and 2005, there were only ten. Oman, Botswana, and Equatorial Guinea are special cases in that large oil or diamond reserves were discovered during this period. Singapore and Hong Kong are city states, and that makes them special since there was no peasant agricultural sector to swamp the city with migrants when investment rose. Wages could, therefore, increase in step with labour demand, and prosperity could spread. The interesting cases are the large countries with large agricultural sectors – Japan, South Korea, Taiwan, Thailand, and China. In addition, the Soviet Union could be added since income per head grew at 4.5% per year from 1928 to 1970 if the Second World War decade is left out.

These countries had to close three gaps with the West – in education, capital, and productivity. Mass schooling closed the education gap, and one form or another of state-led industrialization closed the capital and productivity gaps. Large-scale, capital-intensive technologies were adopted even when they were not immediately cost-effective. These countries have avoided the inefficiencies that Latin America has endured in trying to shoe-horn modern technology into small economies either because they were so large that they could absorb the output of efficient facilities or because they were given access to the American market at the expense of American production.

Which of the many initiatives followed by these countries was the most effective, however, remains the subject of a great deal of debate. Also, it is not so clear whether the successful policies can be transplanted to other countries. The best policy to effect economic development, therefore, remains very much in dispute.

References

Chapter 1: The great divergence

Pelsaert: Tapan Raychaudhuri and Irfan Habib, *The Cambridge Economic History of India*, Vol. I, *c. 1200-c. 1750* (Cambridge University Press, 1982), p. 462.

Dr Johnson on oats: Samuel Johnson, *A Dictionary of the English Language* (1755).

$1 per day poverty line: World Bank's *World Development Report: Poverty* (Oxford University Press, 1990); and Martin Ravallion, Datt Gaurav, and Dominique van de Walle, 'Quantifying Absolute Poverty in the Developing World', *Review of Income and Wealth*, 37 (1991): 345–61.

Italian soldiers: Brian A'Hearn, 'Anthropometric Evidence on Living Standards in Northern Italy, 1730–1860', *Journal of Economic History*, 63 (2003): 351–81.

Ealing gardener: Sir Frederick Eden, *The State of the Poor* (J. Davis, 1797), Vol. II, pp. 433–5.

Chapter 3: The Industrial Revolution

efficiency of farmers in poor countries: T. W. Schultz, *Transforming Traditional Agriculture* (Yale University Press, 1964); R. A. Berry and W. R. Cline, *Agrarian Structure and Productivity in Developing Countries* (Johns Hopkins University Press, 1979); Robert C. Allen, *Enclosure and the Yeoman* (Oxford University Press, 1992).

French and British tax burden: P. Mathias and P. K. O'Brien, 'Taxation in England and France, 1715–1810', *Journal of European Economic History*, 5 (1976): 601–50.

Provence: J.-L. Rosenthal, 'The Development of Irrigation in Provence', *Journal of Economic History*, 50 (September 1990): 615–38.

despotic power of Parliament: Julian Hoppit, 'Patterns of Parliamentary Legislation, 1660–1800', *The History Journal*, 39 (1996): 126.

witchcraft and the Bible: John Wesley, *Journal*, for 21 May 1768.

Hobsbawm on cotton: Eric Hobsbawm, *Industry and Empire* (Weidenfeld & Nicolson, 1969), p. 56.

Desaguliers on Newcomen engine: John Theophilus Desaguliers, *A Course of Experimental Philosophy* (John Senex, 1734–44), Vol. II, pp. 464–5.

steam power and productivity growth: N. F. R. Crafts, 'Steam as a General Purpose Technology: A Growth Accounting Perspective', *Economic Journal*, 114 (495) (2004): 338–51.

Chapter 5: The great empires

1812 costs in England and India: Edward Baines, *History of the Cotton Manufacture in Great Britain* (H. Fisher, R. Fisher, and P. Jackson, 1835), p. 353. *First Report from the Select Committee on the Affairs of the East India Company (China Trade)*, UK, House of Commons, 1830 (644), evidence of Mr John Kennedy and Mr H. H. Birley, questions 4979–5041.

decline of weaving in Bihar: Amiya Kumar Bagchi, 'Deindustrialization in Gangetic Bihar, 1809–1901', in Barun De (ed.), *Essays in Honour of Professor S. C. Sakar* (New Delhi, People's Publishing House, 1976), pp. 499–523.

Martin and Brocklehurst: UK House of Commons, *Report from the Select Committee on East India Produce*, 1840 (527), question 3920.

Chapter 6: The Americas

cultivation of maize in eastern North America: Bruce D. Smith, *The Emergence of Agriculture* (Scientific American Library, 1998), pp. 145–81, 200; and Bruce G. Trigger, *The Children of Aataentsic: A History of the Huron People to 1660* (McGill-Queen's University Press, 1987), pp. 119–26.

native population decline: Russell Thornton, *American Indian Holocaust and Survival: A Population History since 1492* (University of Oklahoma Press, 1987), pp. 25, 57, 133.

Mexican and Andean native populations: Mark A. Burkholder and
Lyman L. Johnson, *Colonial Latin America*, 2nd edn. (Oxford
University Press, 1994), p. 264; and James Lockhard and Stuart
B. Schwartz, *Early Latin America: A History of Colonial Spanish
America and Brazil* (Cambridge University Press, 1983), p. 338.

14,697: Thornton, *American Indian Holocaust*, pp. 29, 162–3.

The quotation relating to God and the epidemic of 1617–19 is from John
Eliot, *New England's First Fruits* (Henry Overton, 1643), p. 12.

The quotation about making cloth is from Edward Johnson, *The
Wonder-Working Providence of Sions Saviour, in New England,
1628–1651*, Book II, Chapter XXI at http://puritanism.online.fr/
(accessed 4 April 2011).

exports as a percentage of GDP in Pennsylvania: exports are the sum
of Proud's contemporary estimate of £700,000 per year for
1771–3 plus £161,000, which equals 64% of the estimates of
average annual shipping earnings and invisible earnings of the
middle Atlantic colonies for 1768–72, in James F. Shepherd and
Gary M. Walton, *Shipping, Maritime Trade, and the Economic
Development of Colonial North America* (Cambridge University
Press, 1972), pp. 128, 134. In 1765–7 and 1772, 64% of the
tonnage of shipping clearing New York and Philadelphia came
from the latter. Proud's estimate of exports exceeds Shepherd and
Walton's. GDP equals the 1770 population of 240,100 multiplied
by £12 per head.

Jamaica exports/GDP in 1832: Gisela Eisner, *Jamaica, 1830–1930: A
Study in Economic Growth* (Manchester University Press,
1961), p. 25.

South Carolina's export of skins and cedar: quoted by John J.
McCusker and Russell R. Mennard, *The Economy of British
North America* (University of North Carolina Press, 1985), p. 171.

Carolina rice productivity: Marc Egnal, *New World Economies: The
Growth of the Thirteen Colonies and Early Canada* (Oxford
University Press, 1998), pp. 105–6.

30% ratio of exports to income: per capita exports from Peter A.
Coclanis, *The Shadow of a Dream: Economic Life and Death in the
South Carolina Low Country, 1670–1920* (Oxford University Press,
1989), p. 75, and per capita income (high value) from Alice Hanson
Jones, *Wealth of a Nation To Be: The American Colonies on the Eve
of the Revolution* (Arno Press, 1980), p. 63.

farmers on the frontier buying consumer goods: McCusker and
Mennard, *British North America*, pp. 175, 180–1.

half the land in the valley of Mexico: Charles Gibson, *The Aztecs under Spanish Rule: A History of the Indians of the Valley of Mexico, 1519–1810* (Stanford University Press, 1964), p. 277.

British Columbia seal skins: Alexander von Humboldt, *Political Essay on the Kingdom of New Spain*, tr. John Black (London, 1822), Vol. II, pp. 311, 320.

road from Vera Cruz to Mexico City: von Humboldt, *Political Essay*, Vol. IV, pp. 8–9.

mine employment: Peter Bakewell, 'Mining in Colonial Spanish America', in *The Cambridge History of Latin America*, Vol. II, ed. Leslie Bethell (Cambridge University Press, 1984), pp. 127–8; and Enrique Tandeter, *Coercion and Market: Silver Mining in Colonial Potosi, 1692–1826* (University of New Mexico Press, 1993), p. 16.

The 4% share of exports in Mexican GDP in 1800 is from John H. Coatsworth, 'The Decline of the Mexican Economy, 1800–1860', in *América Latina en la época de Simón Bolívar: la formación de la economías latinoamericanos y los intereses económicos europeos, 1800–1850*, ed. Reinhart Liehr (Berlin, Colloquium Verlag, 1989), p. 51.

income distribution of Mexico in 1790: Branko Milanovic, Peter H. Lindert, and Jeffrey G. Williamson, 'Measuring Ancient Inequality', Cambridge, MA, National Bureau of Economic Research, Working Paper 13550, http://www.nber.org/papers/13550.pdf, 2007, p. 60.

size of national cotton industries in the 1850s: Robert C. Allen, *The British Industrial Revolution in Global Perspective* (Cambridge University Press, 2009), p. 211.

exports to GDP in the USA 1800–60: Susan B. Carter, Scott Sigmund Gartner, Michael R. Haines, Alan L. Olmstead, Richard Sutch, and Gavin Wright, *Historical Statistics of the United States*, millenium edition, online (Cambridge University Press), series Ca10 and Ee366.

de-industrialization in Puebla: von Humboldt, *Political Essay*, Vol. III, p. 469.

scientific culture and education in Mexico: von Humboldt, *Political Essay*, Vol. I, pp. 212, 216, 223.

the spirits of traders: Mary Kingsley, *Travels in West Africa* (National Geographic Society, 2002; originally published 1897), p. 36.

biggest pots: Harold A. Innis, *The Fur Trade in Canada: An Introduction to Canadian Economic History* (University of Toronto Press, 1999; originally published 1930), p. 18.

the Micmac joke: Father Chrestien Le Clercq, in his *New Relation of Gaspesia*, tr. and ed. W. F. Ganong (The Champlain Society, 1910), p. 277.

Alfonso I's letter: quoted by Adam Hochschild, *King Leopold's Ghost: A Story of Greed, Terror, and Heroism in Colonial Africa* (Houghton Mifflin, 1998), p. 13.

Swanzy's testimony: UK, House of Commons, *Report from the Select Committee on the West Coast of Africa*; together with the minutes of evidence, appendix, and index. Part I, *Report and Evidence*, Parliamentary Papers (1842), Vols. XI, XII, questions 467 and 468.

hectares of palm trees in Nigeria: Kenneth F. Kiple and Kriemhild Coneè Ornelas (eds.), *The Cambridge World History of Food* (Cambridge University Press, 2000), section II.E.3, palm oil.

the Reverend Casalis' observation: R. C. Germond (ed.), *Chronicles of Basutoland: A Running Commentary on the Events of the Years 1830–1902 by the French Protestant Missionaries in Southern Africa* (Morija Sesuto Book Depot, 1967), p. 267.

profitability of palm oil extraction: calculated from Eric L. Hyman, 'An Economic Analysis of Small-Scale Technologies for Palm Oil Extraction in Central and West Africa', *World Development*, 18 (1990): 455–76.

Machel 'for the nation to live': quoted by Mahmood Mamdani, *Citizen and Subject* (Princeton University Press, 1996), p. 135.

Chapter 8: The standard model and late industrialization

short men in Tokugawa Japan: Akira Hayami, Osamu Saitô, and Ronald P. Toby (eds.), *Emergence of Economic Society in Japan, 1600–1859* (Oxford University Press, 2004), pp. 235–8.

book rental shops in Edo: Hayami et al., *Emergence*, pp. 28, 241.

MES: James Montgomery, *A Practical Detail of the Cotton Manufacture of the United States of America* (Glasgow, 1840); J. P. Lesley, *The Iron Manufacturer's Guide to the Furnaces, Forges and Rolling Mills of the United States* (New York, 1859); D. G. Rhys, *The Motor Industry: An Economic Survey* (Butterworths, 1972); Jack Baranson, *Automotive Industries in Developing Countries*

(World Bank, 1969); Rich Kronish and Kenneth S. Mericle (eds.), *The Political Economy of the Latin American Motor Vehicle Industry* (MIT Press, 1984); John P. Tuman and John T. Morris (eds.), *Transforming the Latin American Automobile Industry: Unions, Workers, and the Politics of Restructuring* (M. E. Sharpe, 1998); United Nations Report, *A Study of the Iron and Steel Industry in Latin America* (United Nations, 1954).

Chapter 9: Big Push industrialization

Lenin quip: V. I. Lenin, 'Report on the Work of the Council of People's Commissars', Eighth All-Russia Congress of Soviets, 22 December 1920, *Collected Works*, tr. and ed. Julius Katzer, Vol. 31, p. 516.
heights in 1891 and 1976: Takafusa Nakamura, *The Postwar Japanese Economy: Its Development and Structure* (University of Tokyo Press, 1981), p. 96.

Further reading

Chapter 1: The great divergence

Adam Smith, *An Inquiry into the Nature and Causes of the Wealth of Nations* (London, 1776).

Eric Hobsbawm, *The Age of Revolution, 1789–1848* (Phoenix, 1962).

Eric Hobsbawm, *The Age of Capital, 1848–1875* (Phoenix, 1975).

Eric Hobsbawm, *The Age of Empire, 1875–1914* (Phoenix, 1987).

Eric Hobsbawm, *The Age of Extremes: A Short History of the Twentieth Century, 1914–1991* (Phoenix, 1994).

Angus Maddison, *The World Economy* (OECD, 2006).

Lane Pritchett, 'Divergence, Big Time', *Journal of Economic Perspectives*, 11 (1997): 3–17.

Branko Milanovic, *Worlds Apart: Measuring International and Global Inequality* (Princeton University Press, 2005).

Robert W. Fogel, *The Escape from Hunger and Premature Death, 1700–2100* (Cambridge University Press, 2004).

Chapter 2: The rise of the West

Jared Diamond, *Guns, Germs, and Steel* (Jonathan Cape, 1997).

Eric Jones, *The European Miracle* (Cambridge University Press, 1981).

J. M. Blaut, *The Colonizer's Model of the World* (Guildford Press, 1993).

James Robinson and Daron Acemoglu, *Why Nations Fail* (Crown, 2011).

Douglas North, *Institutions, Institutional Change, and Economic Performance* (Cambridge University Press, 1990).

Jan de Vries, *The Industrious Revolution: Consumer Behaviour and the Household Economy, 1650 to the Present* (Cambridge University Press, 2008).

Richard W. Unger, *The Ship in the Medieval Economy: 600–1600* (Croom Helm, 1980).

Joseph E. Inikori, *Africans and the Industrial Revolution in England: A Study in International Trade and Economic Development* (Cambridge University Press, 2002).

Max Weber, *The Protestant Ethic and the Spirit of Capitalism* (Allen & Unwin, 1930).

Robert Putnam, *Making Democracy Work: Civic Traditions in Modern Italy* (Princeton University Press, 1993).

Jan Luiten van Zanden, *The Long Road to the Industrial Revolution: The European Economy in a Global Perspective, 1000–1800* (Brill, 2009).

D. C. North and B. R. Weingast, 'Constitutions and Commitment: Evolution of Institutions Governing Public Choice in Seventeenth Century England', *Journal of Economic History*, 49 (1989): 803–32.

J. Bradford De Long and Andrei Schleifer, 'Princes and Merchants: European City Growth before the Industrial Revolution', *Journal of Law and Economics*, 36 (1993): 671–702.

Daron Acemoglu, Simon Johnson, and James Robinson, 'The Rise of Europe: Atlantic Trade, Institutional Change, and Economic Growth', *American Economic Review*, 95(3) (2005): 546–79.

Robert C. Allen, 'Poverty and Progress in Early Modern Europe', *Economic History Review*, LVI(3) (August 2003): 403–43.

Mauricio Drelichman, 'The Curse of Moctezuma: American Silver and the Dutch Disease', *Explorations in Economic History*, 42 (2005): 349–80.

Chapter 3: The Industrial Revolution

Robert C. Allen, *The British Industrial Revolution in Global Perspective* (Cambridge University Press, 2009).

Joel Mokyr, *The Enlightened Economy: An Economic History of Britain, 1700–1850* (Yale University Press, 2010) offers another interpretation as well as a wide-ranging survey of issues.

Nick Crafts, *British Economic Growth during the Industrial Revolution* (Clarendon Press, 1985).

Jane Humphries, *Childhood and Child Labour in the British Industrial Revolution* (Cambridge University Press, 2010).

Friedrich Engels, *The Condition of the Working Class in England*, tr. and ed. W. O. Henderson (Blackwell, 1958).

Phyllis Deane and W. A. Cole, *British Economic Growth, 1688–1959: Trends and Structure*, 2nd edn. (Cambridge University Press, 1969).

Knick Harley, 'British Industrialization before 1841: Evidence of Slower Growth during the Industrial Revolution', *Journal of Economic History*, 42(1982): 267–89.

Peter Temin, 'Two Views of the British Industrial Revolution', *Journal of Economic History*, 57 (1997): 63–82.

Chapter 4: The ascent of the rich

Stephen Broadberry and Kevin O'Rourke, *The Cambridge Economic History of Modern Europe* (Cambridge University Press, 2010).

David S. Landes, *The Unbound Prometheus: Technological Change and Industrial Development in Western Europe from 1750 to the Present* (Cambridge University Press, 1969).

Patrick K. O'Brien and C. Keyder, *Economic Growth in Britain and France, 1780–1914: Two Paths to the Twentieth Century* (Allen & Unwin, 1978).

Alexander Gerschenkron, *Economic Backwardness in Historical Perspective* (Harvard University Press, 1962).

Ha-Joon Change, *Kicking Away the Ladder: Development Strategy in Historical Perspective* (Anthem, 2002).

Kevin O'Rourke, 'Tariffs and Growth in the Late Nineteenth Century', *Economic Journal*, 110(463) (2000): 456–83.

Robert C. Allen, 'Technology and the Great Divergence', Oxford University, Dept. of Economics, Discussion Paper 548 *Explorations in Economic History* (2012).

Sascha Becker and Ludger Woessmann, 'Was Weber Wrong? A Human Capital Theory of Protestant Economic History', *Quarterly Journal of Economics*, 124 (2009): 531–96.

Chapter 5: The great empires

The California School includes:

Kenneth Pomeranz, *The Great Divergence: China, Europe, and the Making of the Modern World Economy* (Princeton University Press, 2000).

Bozhong Li, *Agricultural Development in Jiangnan, 1620–1850* (Macmillan, 1998).

R. Bin Wong, *China Transformed* (Cornell University Press, 1997).

James Lee and Wang Feng, *One Quarter of Humanity: Malthusian Mythology and Chinese Realities, 1700–2000* (Harvard University Press, 1999).

Jack Goldstone, *Why Europe? The Rise of the West in World History 1500–1850* (McGraw-Hill Higher Education, 2008).

Robert Marks, *The Origins of the Modern World: Fate and Fortune in the Rise of the West* (Rowman & Littlefield, 2006).

Peter Temin, *The Economics of Antiquity* (Princeton University Press, 2012).

Globalization and de-industrialization

Ronald Findlay and Kevin O'Rourke, *Power and Plenty: Trade, War, and the World Economy in the Second Millennium* (Princeton University Press, 2007).

Jeffrey G. Williamson, *Trade and Poverty: When the Third World Fell Behind* (MIT Press, 2011).

C. A. Bayly, *Imperial Meridian: The British Empire and the World, 1780–1830* (Longman, 1989).

K. N. Chaudhuri, *Trade and Civilization in the Indian Ocean* (Cambridge University Press, 1985).

Tirthanakar Roy, *The Economic History of India, 1857–1947* (Oxford University Press, 2006).

Daniel R. Headrick, *The Tentacles of Progress: Technology Transfer in the Age of Imperialism, 1850–1940* (Oxford University Press, 1988).

Nelly Hanna, *Making Big Money in 1600: The Life and Times of Isma'il Abu Taqiyya, Egyptian Merchant* (Syracuse University Press, 1988).

Robert Brenner, *Property and Progress: The Historical Origins and Social Foundations of Self-Sustaining Growth* (Verso, 2009).

John Darwin, *After Tamerlane: The Rise and Fall of Global Empires, 1400–2000* (Penguin, 2008).

Perry Anderson, *Passages from Antiquity to Feudalism* (Verso, 1996).

Niall Ferguson, *Empire: How Britain Made the Modern World* (Penguin, 2004).

Chris Wickham, *The Inheritance of Rome* (Penguin, 2010).

Chapter 6: The Americas

Bruce D. Smith, *The Emergence of Agriculture* (Scientific American Library, 1998).

Russell Thornton, *American Indian Holocaust and Survival: A Population History since 1492* (University of Oklahoma Press, 1987).

J. H. Elliott, *Empires of the Atlantic World: Britain and Spain in America, 1492–1830* (Yale University Press, 2006).

Harold A. Innis, *The Fur Trade in Canada* (Yale University Press, 1930).

Stanley L. Engerman and Kenneth L. Sokoloff, *Economic Development in the Americas since 1500: Endowments and Institutions* (Cambridge University Press, 2012).

John J. McCusker and Russell R. Menard, *The Economy of British America, 1607–1789* (University of North Carolina Press, 1985).

Ann Carlos and Frank Lewis, *Commerce by a Frozen Sea: Native Americans and the European Fur Trade* (University of Pennsylvania Press, 2010).

Marc Egnal, *New World Economies: The Growth of the Thirteen Colonies and Early Canada* (Oxford University Press, 1998).

Peter A. Coclanis, *The Shadow of a Dream: Economic Life and Death in the South Carolina Low Country, 1670–1920* (Oxford University Press, 1989).

Winifred Barr Rothenberg, *From Market-Places to the Market Economy: The Transformation of Rural Massachusetts, 1750–1850* (University of Chicago Press, 1992).

On technology in the USA

H. J. Habakkuk, *American and British Technology in the Nineteenth Century* (Cambridge University Press, 1962).

Paul A. David, *Technical Choice, Innovation, and Economic Growth: Essays on American and British Experience in the Nineteenth Century* (Cambridge University Press, 1975).

Peter Temin, 'Labor Scarcity and the Problem of American Industrial Efficiency in the 1850s', *Journal of Economic History*, 26 (1966): 277–98.

Peter Temin, 'Notes on Labor Scarcity in America', *Journal of Interdisciplinary History*, 1 (1971): 251–64.

David A. Hounshell, *From the American System to Mass Production, 1800–1932* (Johns Hopkins University Press, 1984).

Gavin Wright, 'The Origins of American Industrial Success, 1879–1940', *American Economic Review*, 80(1990): 651–68.

Richard R. Nelson and Gavin Wright, 'The Rise and Fall of American Technological Leadership: The Postwar Era in Historical Perspective', *Journal of Economic Literature*, 30(1992): 1931–64.

Naomi R. Lamoreaux, Daniel M. G. Raff, and Peter Temin (eds.), *Learning by Doing in Markets, Firms, and Countries* (University of Chicago Press, 1999).

Alan Olmstead and Paul Rohde, *Creating Abundance: Biological Innovation and American Agricultural Development* (Cambridge University Press, 2008).

On the economics of slavery

Robert Fogel and Stanley Engerman, *Time on the Cross: The Economics of American Negro Slavery* (Little Brown, 1974).

Paul A. David, Herbert G. Gutman, Richard Sutch, Peter Temin, and Gavin Wright, *Reckoning with Slavery* (Oxford University Press, 1976).

Roger Ransom and Richard Sutch, *One Kind of Freedom: The Economic Consequences of Emancipation* (Cambridge University Press, 1977).

Gavin Wright, *Old South, New South: Revolutions in the Southern Economy since the Civil War* (Basic Books, 1986).

On Latin America

Mark A. Burkholder and Lyman L. Johnson, *Colonial Latin America*, 2nd edn. (Oxford University Press, 1994).

James Lockhart and Stuart B. Schwartz, *Early Latin America: A History of Colonial Spanish America and Brazil* (Cambridge University Press, 1983).

Charles Gibson, *The Aztecs under Spanish Rule* (Stanford University Press, 1964).

Alan Knight, *Mexico: The Colonial Era* (Cambridge University Press, 2002).

John H. Coatsworth, 'Obstacles to Economic Growth in Nineteenth Century Mexico', *The American Historical Review*, 83(1978): 80–100.

Victor Bulmer-Thomas, John Coatsworth, and Roberto Cortés Conde (eds.), *The Cambridge Economic History of Latin America* (Cambridge University Press, 2006).

Chapter 7: Africa

E. Domar, 'The Causes of Slavery and Serfdom: A Hypothesis', *Journal of Economic History*, 30(1970): 18–32.

Walter Rodney, *How Europe Underdeveloped Africa* (Howard University Press, 1982).

Paul Collier, *The Bottom Billion* (Oxford University Press, 2008).

Robert H. Bates, *Beyond the Miracle of the Market: The Political Economy of Agrarian Development in Kenya* (Cambridge University Press, 1989).

Hans Ruthenberg, *Farming Systems in the Tropics*, 2nd edn. (Clarendon Press, 1976).

Ester Boserup, *The Conditions of Agricultural Growth* (Allen & Unwin, 1965).

Charles H. Feinstein, *An Economic History of South Africa: Conquest, Discrimination and Development* (Cambridge University Press, 2005).

R. S. O'Fahey, *The Darfur Sultanate: A History* (Hurst, 2008).

Roland Dumont, Alexandre Dansi, Philippe Vernier, and Jeanne Zoundjihèkpon, *Biodiversity and Domestication of Yams in West Africa: Traditional Practices Leading to Dioscorea Rotundata Poir* (CIRAD, 2005).

Angus Deaton, 'Commodity Prices and Growth in Africa', *Journal of Economic Perspectives*, 13(1999): 23–40.

Kojo Sebastian Amanor, *The New Frontier: Farmers' Response to Land Degredation, A West African Study* (UNRSID, 1994).

Kojo Sebastian Amanor and Sam Moyo (eds.), *Land and Sustainable Development in Africa* (Zed Books, 2008).

Terence Ranger, 'The Invention of Tradition in Colonial Africa', in Eric Hobsbawm and Terence Ranger (eds.), *The Invention of Tradition* (Cambridge University Press, 1983), pp. 211–62.

Randall M. Packard, *The Making of a Tropical Disease: A Short History of Malaria* (Johns Hopkins University Press, 2007).

Michael Havinden and David Meredith, *Colonialism and Development: Britain and its Tropical Colonies, 1850–1960* (Routledge, 1993).

Marshall Sahlins, *Stone Age Economics* (Aldine de Gruyter, 1972).

James C. McCann, *Maize and Grace: Africa's Encounter with a New World Crop, 1500–2000* (Harvard University Press, 2005).

A. G. Hopkins, *An Economic History of West Africa* (Longman, 1973).

Jan Vansina, *Paths in the Rainforests: Toward a History of Political Tradition in Equatorial Africa* (Currey, 1990).

Mahmood Mamdani, *When Victims Become Killers: Colonialism, Nativism, and the Genocide in Rwanda* (Princeton University Press, 2001).

Patrick Manning, *Slavery and African Life* (Cambridge University Press, 1990).

Mahmood Mamdani, *Citizen and Subject: Contemporary Africa and the Legacy of Late Colonialism* (Princeton University Press, 1996).

Polly Hill, *The Migrant Cocoa Farmers of Southern Ghana: A Study in Rural Capitalism* (Cambridge University Press, 1963).

Gareth Austin, *Labour, Land and Capital in Ghana: From Slavery to Free Labour in Asante, 1807–1956* (University of Rochester Press, 2005).

Benno J. Ndulu, Stephen A. O'Connell, Robert H. Bates, Paul Collier, and Chukwuma C. Soludo, *The Political Economy of Economic Growth in Africa, 1960–2000* (Cambridge University Press, 2008).

Gerald K. Helleiner, *Peasant Agriculture, Government, and Economic Growth in Nigeria* (Richard D. Irwin, 1966).

Chapter 8: The standard model and late industrialization

Peter Gatrell, *The Tsarist Economy: 1850–1917* (St Martin's Press, 1986).

M. E. Falkus, *The Industrialisation of Russia: 1700–1914* (Economic History Society, 1972).

Susan B. Hanley and Kozo Yamamura, *Economic and Demographic Change in Pre-Industrial Japan, 1600–1868* (Princeton University Press, 1977).

Akira Hayami, Osamu Saitô, and Ronald P. Roby (eds.), *Emergence of Economic Society in Japan, 1600–1859* (Oxford University Press, 1999).

Thomas C. Smith, *The Agrarian Origins of Modern Japan* (Stanford University Press, 1959).

Tessa Morris-Suzuki, *The Technological Transformation of Japan from the Seventeenth to the Twenty-First Century* (Cambridge University Press, 1994).

Keijiro Utsuka, Gustav Ranis, and Gary Saxonhouse, *Comparative Technology Choice in Development: The Indian and Japanese Cotton Textile Industries* (St Martin's Press, 1988).

Yujiro Hayami and Vernon W. Ruttan, *Agricultural Development: An International Perspective* (Johns Hopkins University Press, 1971).

Victor Bulmer-Thomas, *An Economic History of Latin America since Independence* (Cambridge University Press, 1994).

Rosemary Thorp, *Progress, Poverty and Exclusion: An Economic History of Latin America in the 20th Century* (Inter-American Development Bank, 1988).

Chapter 9: Big Push industrialization

Robert C. Allen, *Farm to Factory: A Reinterpretation of the Soviet Industrial Revolution* (Princeton University Press, 2003).

Holland Hunter and Janusz M. Szyrmer, *Faulty Foundations: Soviet Economic Policies, 1928–1940* (Princeton University Press, 1992).

R. W. Davies, Mark Harrison, and S. G. Wheatcroft, *The Economic Transformation of the Soviet Union, 1913–1945* (Cambridge University Press, 1994).

The World Bank, *East Asian Miracle: Economic Growth and Public Policy* (Oxford University Press, 1993).

Christopher Howe, *The Origins of Japanese Trade Supremacy* (Chicago University Press, 1996).

Chalmers A. Johnson, *MITI and the Japanese Miracle: The Growth of Industrial Policy, 1925–1975* (Stanford University Press, 1982).

Alice H. Amsden, *The Rise of 'The Rest': Challenges to the West from Late-Industrializing Economies* (Oxford University Press, 2001).

Barry Naughton, *The Chinese Economy: Transitions and Growth* (MIT Press, 2007).

Loren Brandt and Thomas G. Rawski (eds.), *China's Great Economic Transformation* (Cambridge University Press, 2008).

Index

Index

Expand your collection of
VERY SHORT INTRODUCTIONS

ECONOMICS
A Very Short Introduction
Partha Dasgupta

Economics has the capacity to offer us deep insights into
some of the most formidable problems of life, and offer
solutions to them too. Combining a global approach with
examples from everyday life, Partha Dasgupta describes the
lives of two children who live very different lives in different
parts of the world: in the Mid-West USA and in Ethiopia. He
compares the obstacles facing them, and the processes that
shape their lives, their families, and their futures. He shows
how economics uncovers these processes, finds explanations
for them, and how it forms policies and solutions.

'An excellent introduction ... presents mathematical and statistical
findings in straightforward prose.'

Financial Times

GLOBALIZATION
A Very Short Introduction
Manfred Steger

'Globalization' has become one of the defining buzzwords of our time – a term that describes a variety of accelerating economic, political, cultural, ideological, and environmental processes that are rapidly altering our experience of the world. It is by its nature a dynamic topic – and this *Very Short Introduction* has been fully updated for 2009, to include developments in global politics, the impact of terrorism, and environmental issues. Presenting globalization in accessible language as a multifaceted process encompassing global, regional, and local aspects of social life, Manfred B. Steger looks at its causes and effects, examines whether it is a new phenomenon, and explores the question of whether, ultimately, globalization is a good or a bad thing.

www.oup.com/vsi